Repossess Your Life!

...

5 Steps for Creating a Lifetime of Success

...

Kayton B Kimberly

This publication is designed to provide accurate and authoritative information in regard to the subject matter covered. It is published with the understanding that the publisher and author are not engaged in rendering legal, medical, or other professional service. If professional advice is required, the services of a competent professional person should be sought. - *From a Declaration of Principles, jointly adopted by a Committee of the American Bar Association and a Committee of Publishers.*

Published GHD Publishers, LLC
Copyright © 2004- 2008 by Kayton B Kimberly

All rights reserved. No part of this book may be produced or transmitted in any form or by any means, electronic or mechanical, including photocopying, recording, or by any information storage and retrieval system, without permission in writing from the author or publisher.
Library of Congress Cataloging-in-Publication Data
Kimberly,Kayton B
    Repossess Your Life / Kayton B Kimberly.--- 1st pbk. Ed.

ISBN   978-0-6151-9881-1

Dedication

To my wife Danielle, who never stops believing in what I can achieve. To my dad, who gave me the knowledge to help others find what they've been looking for. To my brother, whose strength is in helping others.

In addition, this book is dedicated to my mom and Josh, who have a great view of everything I do. Lastly, to my friend Claudia and our great night in Tampa.

CONTENTS

CHAPTER 1	A PARABLE OF SUCCESS	1
CHAPTER 2	SUCCESS-WHAT IS AND ISN'T	9
CHAPTER 3	THE 90% CLUB A PLACE FOR THE HAVE-NOTS	35
CHAPTER 4	THE OTHER 10%	61
CHAPTER 5	1,2,3 TOO MANY (HOW YOUR BRAIN WORKS)	81
CHAPTER 6	THE 10% SOLUTION (THE ALADDIN'S LAMP TO YOUR PROBLEMS)	117
CHAPTER 7	THE POWER OF WHY	129
CHAPTER 8	ITS TIME TO BE	143
CHAPTER 9	BEGINNING THE 5 STEPS	159
CHAPTER 10	THE 5 STEPS FOR LIFELONG SUCCESS	163
CHAPTER 11	BEYOND TODAY	187

"There are some people who live in a dream world, and there are some who face reality; and then there are those who turn one into the other."

- Douglas Everett

Chapter 1
A Parable of Success

It's four in the morning on another steamy summers night. The drunks, lovers and dreamers have all but settled into their own moments of desire. A stale stench of sex, beer and cigarette smoke hover over this town like the darkness beyond its dimly light skyline. As the night slowly gives away it's virginity to the promise of a day which is new, one more act of passion will take place.

Poised at the crossroads of chance, a man thinks about his next move. Within the shadows of these city streets images of a future yet to come, play out in his mind. Who is this man?

His living is based on a hard reality of broken dreams. Like millions of others the world around, he shares in a reality of scarcity, of not enough money and not enough time. Alone he stands pondering the question of *if there were only more*. With a sigh, he exhales and eyes a metal beast that lies silent in its lair.

The man emerges from the shadows. In his hand a cold metal key. He walks the small stretch of pavement between him and destiny, and with the exactness of a surgeon, cuts the key into the ignition. In an instant, the blue giant is brought from its slumber. Groaning in defiance, it backs out of the driveway. For the moment, all is well. No shots ring out. No blood is spilled. Then it happens.

Lights from a living room fill the lawn as the front door is opened and in the doorway, a silhouette yells threats to a now deaf ear. Smiling in nervous confidence the man gases the blue beast hard. Somewhere in the fumes of exhaust and rubber burning, he spies two arms flailing in the air. It's yet another feeble attempt at stopping him, the third this week. Driving on instinct and an empty tank, he speeds away. Nothing can change what has transpired. The moment is done. This *"repo-man"* has had another success, another car of many for this Urban Robin Hood. The games of early morning darkness are erased by the slow creeping of dawns light.

As the rest of the world comes to life, he'll start a conversation with those who hired to say, "All is well." At that instant, someone will be happy and his name will be praised around an office. At about the same time, the car's former owner will look out into an empty carport and curse the unknown man who took what he thought was his.

Within the moments of today, this process will be repeated a thousand times. In similar fashion, so will the process many call <u>*"success."*</u>

For one, success will become a way to live, a means to provide for his family. For another, it will be an excuse, a way to blame all the wrongs of the world for his despair. One person will take risks, and within those ventures, he will find the rewards of life. The other will do nothing but wait for things to happen. And inside those occurrences, he will profess how unlucky he is.

This is life, and this is the irony of success:_for one it becomes freedom; for another, a prison_. Each one of us can have it all or lose it all. *It becomes a matter of choice.* That is what success is, and the "choice" that we have is what this book is about.

Inside these pages, you will *repossess your life*. You will learn how to walk up the driveway of your destiny and drive your soul to success. You don't need to be mysterious or even smart; *you just have to be willing to be honest.* If you can do that, then this book may be the turning point your life has been in need of.

I write in "need of" for a simple reason. Chances are you've been exposed to some person you envisioned as your new "guru." For example, you may have read another book and tried to attain the success that the authority promised, but ended up being disappointed, without your dream in hand. I know that this has been true of me. Often I was promised disclosure about the great secrets that lay behind the attaining of wealth. What I got many times instead was a vague rendering of fact. What I wanted was truth. And when I finally found it, this truth would lead me to find this thing called "success". We all need the truth. We need to discover the honesty of our lives as we see it, not as others perceive it to be. So many experts don't want to tell you that the truth of success is within you, for it's hard for them to sell you on yourself. It's much more profitable to sell you an idea that will make your life easier.

But you don't need another idea; there are plenty of ideas around that are easily available to you. What you need are tools for success. Things that can bring you closer to what you want. And that's where I come in.

I will be the first tell you that I am no guru. I have no super powers either. I don't own a magic wand that will put millions of dollars in your pocket overnight. Yet, in the pages to follow, I can present you with tools for getting the success you want. And the first step in getting to those tools is honesty.

From a place of honesty, we find truth. When we find something to be true, it then becomes easier to believe. It's from a level of belief that things happen. Think of the times you first rode a bike or tied your shoes. After a while you began to believe you could, and so you did. *Believing in things gives us a way to see things without fear.* My wish for you is to begin to see success with that same precision.

With that desire, there are important ideas that you will need to understand. First, contrary to popular belief, success is not a magical point in time when all of your worries dissipate into thin air. When you have success, you will still be experiencing worries. Second, it is critical to understand that success is not measured by the car you drive or the place you live. Success isn't so much about what we do but *who we are.*

Who you are as a person is what brings success. This little fact is missed by the millions who spend their hard-earned money on books about so-called "secrets" of success. With their words, many authors have created a tradition about success and what it takes to get it. And I admit I am guilty of buying into most of these practices. Like many others, I have picked up the latest trendy book about success. Within such book's glossy pages and through its slick title, the authors tell rags- to-riches stories. The idea of success that they sell is what I call *"success osmosis,"* for what they are suggesting is that through the miracle of publishing anyone reading their words will experience the same success. And that's not true.

Another myth I will share is the "tape program." The idea proclaimed here is that by driving along and listening to audio tapes, one's "situation" could improve. By *merely listening* to the great words of inspiration, success will flow from the speakers into the lives of all. Sound familiar?

I fell for these myths at first as well. But when I exhausted my belief in those ideas of success, I bought into the greatest hoax of all: Time. In buying into a "time management system," (fancy words for a calendar) I was sold on the idea that somewhere with my "important" quadrants and "life circles" (or squares) was my success.

I came to realize that though many of these tools were important, that some actually worked, there was still something missing from all of them.

As time passed and being unable to discover the "success" that was promised to me from these myriad of products and "gurus", I began to question its being. - *Did success exist and if so, how could I get it?*

You may have questioned the existence of success as well, and you may even be doing that now; isn't that the reason you picked up this book? You have seen what others around you have and you want to know *how they did it.* But what is success to you?

Perhaps it's that new BMW in the showroom or that sense of peace you notice in the lives of others. *Only you know the answer,* for success is as diverse as those who want it. Each of us may have a different idea, but we all want the same thing: *no one wants to fail.* We are all striving to be unique and success, no matter the level we are hoping to achieve, provides us with that distinction.

It's those distinctions that create these invisible lines of prosperity. Though we can not see them, they are there in an ever present way. They become the dividing marker between social classes. Stepping stones into which one dines seaside or to the other extreme, out of a dumpster. It's a separating line that many believe comes from finding a single answer. As with the famous line from *Field of Dreams, "if you build they will come,"* we lead our lives seeking out concepts that will set us free, wanting the one idea that will make us millionaires or for others, just "better people." I'm no different.

Over a time frame of 18 years, I read books from so-called experts. Like you are doing now, I reached out to find that one unique idea that would make everything work. That hope morphed from reading books to attending seminars. Once I discovered that "live versions" of success were available to me, I became even more enthralled in my passion. My new mission in life was to find it at every turn, and I transformed from a person seeking excellence into a "self-help junkie." The "fix" I needed was from these dealers in success.

Like an addict, I had to have larger and larger hits to satisfy my ever-growing need for a new high. I would fork over hundreds, even thousands of dollars, for the guru's next seminar. I gave into the temptation to buy the tapes or snagged a reader's copy of the guru's next book. My reasoning was simple: I wanted to find the secrets that no one else could and these precious inventions could give me the life I wanted. When it came to discovering success… you name it, I did it. But through it all, "success" evaded me. *Why?*

That is what the rest of this book is for. *In telling you of why success eluded me, I was able to produce strategies to capture it.* Within those ways, I was also able to find sincerity within myself. This honesty provided me with the fuel to use what worked, and to discard what didn't. Being able to distinguish between the two is what brought success to me.

I hope you value and utilize these strategies I've uncovered. However, feel free to utilize all or none; the choice is yours.

But remember that the knowledge gained from this book is limited. *It is constrained to the amount that you exercise it*. If you don't do anything, then you won't achieve anything. So do yourself a favor. Take a chance and use this book as a guide. Create the success that is yours. Stand up and ***repossess your life***!

Chapter 2

Success What Is... and Isn't

Success, according to the Merriam-Webster dictionary, means *a: degree or measure of succeeding; favorable or desired outcome*. It is also defined *as the attainment of wealth, favor, or eminence*.

These definitions are fine if you live in a text-book world. Yet, most of us reside in the real world, a world where success isn't in a dictionary but lies inside a myriad of ideas.

There are books, tapes, and seminars; all designed around one word, "success," and its alleged meaning. The guru's who offer these products claim that success is a "mind set." They attract followers who become "positive thinkers" but as they evolve, they tend to feel that success becomes a reflection of what one does. They start to see themselves as a "successful" people because their "attitude" has now provided them with wealth. Their vocations pay for new cars and even fancier homes in the "nicest parts of town." Their kids get to go to private school and materially speaking, life is *easy*. Then there are those on the other side.

They are the ones who have never read the books or listened to the tapes. The gurus they look up to come in six or twelve packs.

Sure, they feel that someone is successful for what they do, but they come to expect things out of others rather than themselves. They profess things like *"the rich get richer,"* and simply watch as their vocations pay for others' vacations. Believing that "success" is reserved for a lucky few, they go through life financially and spiritually challenged. These thoughts are nothing new.

Take any opportunity or position in life, from being a *stockbroker* to being a *good parent.* There's always someone somewhere who can tell you how to be successful in those ventures. Yet, there are an equal amount of people who will say, *"Those things don't work."* They will be the ones to tell you that *"you can't make money in stocks"* or *"you have to breast feed kids."* Who are we supposed to believe? The experts? Or the non-experts? The ones who have done what it is we want to do? It can be confusing knowing who and what to do. And I discovered in my 18 year pilgrimage to "success", when asked what in fact success is, most would reply with *what it wasn't.*

According to my pastor growing up, success *"wasn't the material things in life."* Yet that idea changed for me when I made some money. I would remember him telling me *"the meek shall inherit the earth." "Well the "meek" didn't drive a Porsche, now did they?"* I thought one day as I pulled out of the Porsche dealership a sunny afternoon shining down upon me.

Success wasn't cheating on a test either. My old high school guidance counselor would tell me, *"It's only the cheaters who fail."* Yet I remember shaking his hand as I grabbed my diploma, all the while hiding behind a nervous smile a dirty little secret I thought I'd never expose. You see, for me, "success" meant graduating from high school and at one point that had entailed paying fifty bucks for answers to an exam. Guilty as charged but too late now.

In those two instances success was not supposed to be everything it turned out to be. Cheaters weren't supposed to win, and the meek were supposed to be happy with the little they had. But I had to prove them wrong. Not for some kind of vindication, but because of my sense of knowing that the world wasn't so black and white. I knew sometimes that cheaters did win; watching a wrestling match proved that. Even the "meek" could own a Porsche… a fact that you can see by watching for my ex-wife smiling as she drives along in traffic. Yet to this day we all still scurry around convincing others of what, exactly, success is. Proving to each other that right is right and wrong is wrong seems to carry some type of significance. *But why?*

I remember playing "house" and "doctor" where the purpose was to pretend. It didn't matter if you were tagged out, burnt the dinner or died from surgery. Success was exploring our youth, imagining silly things and not annoying our parents. Nowadays kids play video games to see who can get the highest score. What has changed? It would seem that success now lies in the outcome, not the imagination.

This new "success formula" seems to be shared by adults as well. Most judge on the outcome, win or lose, and not the practice it took to get there. The truth is that between practice and result lays success for each of us.

The old saying goes "practice makes perfect," but I don't agree. *"Perfect practice makes perfect,"* as said by coach Bear Bryant, better describes what success is to me. It opens up the truth behind an out-dated dogma that many have bought into. Success for many is a concept of "if" and "when." "If I get this, then I can do this" or "When I get this, then I can do this." Success for many is waiting to take all of these steps (or practice) and then get a result. But the opposite is true.

Perfect practice makes perfect means that everything in and of itself is a result. Each step is made towards the end result, whatever that "end" is and that the steps taken have to be consistent with desired result. In other words, the way to get "perfect" is to start with "perfect." Since many know that perfection is subjective, why set ourselves up to lose? Fact is you don't have to, if you realize that success comes from looking at each step as a successful result in and of itself. This was a lesson taught to me in my "earlier" years.

My First Lesson in Success

It was September 1982. That summer had been memorable not for going into the seventh grade, but for being accepted onto the football team. Another thing that stuck out in my mind that year was the rain. It never seemed to stop. We were about a month into the school year and playing our fourth football game against some school notorious for beating us. Then again, that was nothing new: Most schools were known for beating us.

But that little fact didn't seem to bother many of us. Ignorant to how unskilled we were, we practiced from mid- July through September in the hot Florida sun. Our coaches' drove us to run better and faster but that training didn't seem to stick when it came to competition. We had lost every game so far, and the day of the fourth game appeared to be no different. We took the field on that afternoon as we had three times earlier over as many weeks.

Yet something was different about this day. There was a spark. A sense of "team" that wasn't there before. By the time of the first quarter was over we were down 14-0. However, change was in store for us come the second quarter. Not by our playing, but by the weather.

As the whistle blew, a dark ominous cloud came in over the field. In the flash of a bolt of lightning, the heavens opened up. This was not a mere shower, but a storm to rival any bible story written.

When halftime came, we were soaked from the rain and sore from the beating that had been bestowed upon us. Huge chunks of hail were falling from the sky and the wind drove the stinging rain into our eyes. My team walked to the locker room knowing that either another speech would greet us, or the game was going to be cancelled. Either one was no worse than the 35-0 score which was being broadcast to the five people sitting in the stands.

I was one of the last to enter the locker room. Before I could even get my helmet off, one of my teammates ran over to me and said, *"Screw the coach, screw the refs, we're going to play this game."* I looked at him like he was insane. No way were we going to go against the coach or the referees! After all, if they wanted to cancel the game, that was their choice. We were kids... kids who were going to get into a lot more trouble if we "defied authority."

Yet as our coach emerged from his office with a cigarette in hand and a towel around his neck, the decision had already been made by several of our players. We were playing, come hell or high water (which we had both of). Before our coach could say, *"Get your gear off, games over,"* we stormed out of the locker room. *"So much for logical thinking!"* I told myself as I followed my teammates out the door.

Two kids from the school band ran to the other locker room, their mission- to tell the other team that *we were still playing.* By the time the coaches and refs got back to the field, we were running plays like the game was still on. The rain kept falling. The scoreboard was still lit. I noticed that there were 3 minutes left of halftime still. It didn't matter. We didn't care. We were playing as if the third quarter had begun.

But as set as we were on performing, the adults were as firm in the game ending.

I remember a lot of screaming by the ref's, the coaches and the five people in the stands. Many were saying, *"The game is over; keep playing and you'll be suspended."* There were threats of detention going around. I don't believe many of us heard or cared about what the grown-ups had to say. We wanted to play, and that was what we were doing. After about 5 minutes of this chaos surrounding us, the rain seemed to lessen. With the softer drops now bouncing off the flooded field, the game went on.

To this day I don't know who swayed the coaches or the officials' decision. I only know their decision changed.

In the third quarter, I was called off the bench. *"Kimberly, get in there,"* erupted from the man wearing red polyester shorts and dangling a Marlboro from his mouth.

"You got it coach," sprang from lips as I rushed onto the muddy battlefield.

My job was to keep this huge kid from tackling our runner. Within a second, the play happened. Our quarterback handed the ball off and this giant came running towards him. With the rain, the wind and my heart pumping, I ran to intercept. He never saw me coming. His eyes were focused on the runner while mine were on him. I slammed into his side, propelling both our bodies into a field of mud and sod. The water and we both lay there as the sky grumbled dropping its remains onto our helmets. A moment later, a band playing and our cheerleaders screaming broke this seeming solitude. Our team had scored.

The game ended, 42-6. We walked off the field like we had won, even though the score said otherwise. I remember smiling and laughing with my friends. I remember talking about how we had kept playing when everyone had said to stop. I remember a lot of that, for earning plenty of "reflection time" during detention. (sometimes defiance does come at a cost).

Nevertheless, the truth was we had scored. That's what had meant the most to us. We had won the game of not playing by others' rules. *That was what the success of that moment was about.*

We didn't do what we had done to win a game or to go undefeated in a season. We didn't care about championships. "Practicing" for months in the hot Florida sun hadn't been about turning us into gridiron champions, no amount of practice could have made us better. No amount of practice could have changed the truth that on one rainy day in 1982, we would score 6 points and I would help do it. Yet success was mine for I felt great about that day. No amount of practice made that day perfect for me, just the love of a game and a few friends did.

Could I expect you to feel the same success? No, I couldn't. That was one of my days in the sun (or clouds, as it were), my magic moment. Success is different things to different people. That's where the success of many first has to be found: <u>from a basic understanding that we are all different.</u> It was that lesson which in a future time would remind me that if we do not learn the lessons at first, they will keep repeating themselves until we do. Success steps can be learned once or over a lifetime, I suggest you learn them once so life doesn't keep giving them to you over and over.

<u>The Universe, a friend, a most valuable lesson</u>

Have you ever had a friend or someone you know go through a *tough time?* For me, his name was, well will call him "Scott" to protect his image.

At the time of *Scotts challenge*, I was doing well and decided to help him out. Offering, I generously signed a lease on an apartment for him. My friend at first did not want to accept my offer because of pride. Typical response by most, right? However, he did so, after my promise to pay half the rent, for the agreement we made included me being able to store some valuable furniture there. He was out of a job, but would be okay with paying half the rent until "he got back on his feet".

On paper the situation seemed that it would benefit us both. Storing the furniture at a storage facility would have cost me more than my half of the apartment's rent. And since my name was on the lease, I could also stop by use the pool or gym that was located at the complex. As for my friend, he was getting a roof over his head without having to come up with any cash first. There was no first, last, security deposits needed. A promise and a handshake was all we did to seal our agreement. It was one of those "win/win" deals I had learned from a seminar somewhere.

With the lease signed, my friend moved in. Over the next few days, I moved some of the furniture (I had made this plan for) into the place as well. Things appeared to be going fine. He was happy to have a place to call home. I was glad to have my furniture not being destroyed by (at the time) my soon- to- be- ex-wife. It was all *"hunky dory"* as they say. But as they also say, *"Appearances can be deceiving."*

With the first month passing and my friend still unemployed I found myself paying the full amount of rent (not the half we agreed) . *"It not so bad,"* I thought. *"In these times it takes months for people to get jobs."*

Success Side Note 1 - Success *is limited by the* **Justifications** *we make!*

The first step many of us take towards limiting the amount of success we obtain is that we reason, we make valid "justifications."

We look at the overall situation of the world and how events of our lives fit into it. As with my friend, I reasoned that he didn't have a job because the market was so tough, so I paid the first month's rent, no questions asked. *Back to the story…*

As the next 30 days passed, I watched with less enthusiasm as my friend worked harder on his tan than getting a job. There was a situation unfolding now that one could not deny. It was going to be two months in a row of my paying the full rent. Two months of paying for an apartment that I had never slept in.

But beyond the financial aspect of that, there was another disturbing trend unfolding. The clean apartment that was a shining example of pride the first month was now a *"pig sty."* And as I looked around the apartment at the half empty food containers and piles of dirty laundry, I noticed the furniture that I was so careful to create this elaborate plan for was being used. His oversized TV was atop my mid -1800's chest. My set of Victorian chairs was doubling as a towel dryer and shoe rack. This was not turning out to be the great solution I thought it would be.

He assured me that a job and the full rent for the third month were nearby.

Looking back, maybe it was that little bit of encouragement that I needed. Hearing my friend tell me he was going to do "something" was a good start. Whatever it was, I thought the third month was not going to be a problem. We were friends, and my belief was that friends would not lie to each other. I was wrong.

About the time the third months rent was due, I received a call from the leasing office. The pleasant voice on the other end told me that, *"I needed to drop the rent check off or get my stuff out."* She then went on to tell me that my neighbors could not stand the late night music that "I" was playing. As if that weren't enough, I was also going to be getting a bill from an exterminator. Seems the adjoining apartments were experiencing a roach infestation caused by "my" refuse collection. I sat there with my cell phone in hand, dumb founded. I couldn't believe it.

By the leasing office I stopped and paid rent for a third month. After that, finding my "friend" and telling him that *"this was not going to work" became* a priority.

I knew of the one place where he would always go back too. When he answered the door, I plunged in using classic lines like, *"How would you feel if..."* and *"Why would you do such a thing?"*

After all my griping, complaining and even yelling, he uttered six words that changed my life. The words uttered from my friend were, *"Kayton, that's your idea of success."*

It took a while (about 3 seconds) to let those profound words sink in and make the realization that my own rules and beliefs were just that, mine alone.

Success Side Note 2- *Success is indeed our own idea. The Universe in all its wisdom, the lessons from earlier and yet again later in life repeated that* <u>Success is our own ideas expressed outwards.</u>

For the truth was, my friend didn't care if he worked or not. He also told me that he was jealous that I owned a successful company. In his eyes, *"I didn't have to work"* and my employees did my work for me. Seemed his perspective on life was jaded in some other areas as well.

With all of the "success" I seemed to have, he found it perfectly justifiable that I pay his way. He frankly didn't believe that he had been taking advantage of me.

But something else was troubling him as well. *He felt, that my life painted such a grandiose picture of success that it left him not knowing where he could begin to make a success of his own life.*

His challenges were many when compared to mine at the time. He wasn't qualified to earn much beyond minimum wage. He had never lived in a place that required its tenants to be quiet and responsible. In his eyes my life was this great example of what was possible, but deep down inside of himself he held a belief that it was "impossible" for him to achieve the same. With this hopeless attitude, he thought, *"Why even try, besides, Kayton could afford it."*

My friend had given up on trying before he ever started! What had transpired was that *I had given my friend the <u>illusion of success, rather than success itself</u>*. I had showed him *the trappings of* success, but not the *secrets behind* the success. I had done nothing to encourage him to be a success himself; I had thought being an example of one was enough (this was my own idea or Belief). That was what had worked for me: every "guru" I had read about was influencing my life somehow, some way. But I had other expectations as well.

In my need for acceptance and recognition, I had come to believe that if I helped enough people, I would be recognized as a "great person." By giving to those around me (like my friend), I had assumed that they would then see beyond the "things" (the money, the cars) of success to the person creating it. For what I was searching for was a *feeling of success*, and not the "things" (the cars, money, etc) that were the result of working towards success.

And for me, part of that "feeling" of success that I was so desperate to achieve included a feeling of acceptance. I wanted acceptance for the person I was, and not for what I did. I kept waiting for my actions to spark my own inner success, and to have others recognize me, not as the career-driven character I was playing.

But that moment had never come. *Had I given up somewhere along the way, like my friend?* No. I was driven because I believed that it was possible and achievable *as long as I didn't stop trying to find success.*

That lesson was taught to me at the cost of a friendship. <u>Has there been a similar event in your life?</u>

<u>Have you experienced a friendship lost over pride or a silly comment?</u> Take a moment and recall an association that was dissolved. Well, somewhere inside your memory should be the reasons the event happened, as well as beliefs about the event. Things like, *"That person hurt me"* or *"They didn't listen to what I had to say"* may resound as responses to a subconscious question. Yet whatever the relationship that dissolved, be it a school yard acquaintance or a marriage of twenty years, the real reason it no longer exists boils down to two factors; *beliefs* and *rules*.

When a relationship fails, it is a matter of your beliefs and rules being violated. To have "conflict" means that both of these two factors are at play.

For example, say you are <u>reading something in a newspaper</u> about a group of people. This group lives in a part of the world where it's acceptable to play loud music twenty-four hours a day. Does this idea "bother" you in any way? Your answer may be yes, no, or maybe. The fact is somewhere in each of us we think that, *"as long as it doesn't bother "me", what do I care what other people do?"* We support this belief by calling it many things, whether saying that it's showing respect for what others honor or being sociable.

Well let me ask you this. What if you lived next door to that loud, music-playing group? What if it was your window their music was blasting in at 3 a.m.? What if it was happening on a night when you had to get some sleep for an important meeting the next day? Would you now have a problem with these music-loving people? Sure. It now "becomes" an issue because these people are living in your own backyard, bombarding your ears with *Kid Rock* at all hours of the day. That belief you had of letting others "do what they want" has all of a sudden come into conflict with your own rules.

Your belief was okay when you sat back, read an article, and gave no thought to things that weren't going on around you. Yet when your belief had to deal with your own space, one of your "rules" determined that *"Hey, maybe I don't want this group in my back yard."* In this example, your belief in having others do what they want and being able to play music loudly is not as much of a priority suddenly as the "rules" you have surrounding that belief. This is why I say both elements must be present to have a disagreement.

Success Side Note 3 - *When you have a disagreement you aren't <u>"fighting"</u> with the other person, but are having <u>a difference when it comes to rules and beliefs</u>*

In all of its diverse meaning, success is a result of beliefs and rules. Who makes up these beliefs and rules? You do. You decide what success is to you and later in this book I will show you how many of these beliefs and rules have influenced your life. These self "truths" are what will bring forth, or deter, the success you want for your life.

"Self truths" are nothing more than ideas which you can relate your life too. In a sense, they are an identity. If I were to say that *"You are nice,"* your brain would think of all the nice things you've done to deserve such a compliment.

On the other side, if I was to describe to you an unattractive trait in someone else, I may say something like "John is a jerk!" or an **shole!", when I say that, your mind will seek out all the bad things about John it can find.

For in my own journey to be "successful," I created many self-truths that were not empowering. I did many things that, on the surface, seemed to be successful when in reality, they left me empty and full with feelings of failure.

Success Side Note 4- *The Process to Success Results (how beliefs and rules run through your brain) - TBAR*

Thought → Belief (self truth) → Action → Result

Once I understood the process above, life got a lot easier for me. Things became a lot clearer, like the world looks when you clean a window, a little brighter and easier to see the things around you.

Before understanding this process my success, even my happiness was not at the level I wanted it to be. Sure I had the beliefs, the life lessons, even the stacks of books, tapes and seminars under my belt. But it was not working. I did some of the most unusual things. See if you can recognize these behaviors in anyone you may know.

SUCCESS DETRACTORS

*Take credit for all the good and blame all the bad stuff on everyone else.

*Look for an instant return (like give to a charity and expect cheap advertising or floods of business from it)

*Think that everyone must act like or agree with you.

*Judge others on how they look, act, speak or for where they live.

*Think that success is a result of the car you drive, the place you live, etc.

These are just a few of things that on the surface may bring success to people, but overall, in the long run, will deter and even ruin them. I know, for I did everything above and more. My life was a wreck and it took a while to figure out why. It took a while of really seeing things from a different perspective, from asking some tough questions but in the end , it boiled down to this. I realized the "steps I were taking, though productive, were not meaningful. From there I discovered The Process of Success Reversal.

The Process to Success Reversal

Thought→ Action→ Result → Belief (Self Truth)

If your life isn't working the way you want- look at the above formula and compare to the one which does work (Thought- Belief- action- Result). See where you are putting your *actions* and what you *believe* is your *result*.

The most challenging thing I hear is from those whose lives are riddled with "Success Detractors" who tell me *"yes but Kayton look, I made millions of dollars doing things this way, so there fore I am successful"*. My response is *"that success is a belief; there is no right or wrong, however, if you want lasting success, the stuff that grows, that keeps coming, then look at the order you doing things and then get back to me"*. Most don't. Most enjoy getting more and more from life instead of having it taken away. If you are one of the others who want to keep struggling, then this book may not offer you more than entertainment. If you want results, then keep reading.

The truth-be told, *sometimes the hardest person you have to convince is the one whose reflection is in the mirror.* Someone once said of the fighter Mike Tyson, *"The only man that can beat Mike*

Tyson is Mike Tyson." The only person that can defeat you is you. You are the one who will determine what success is in your life. This is true for success or anything else in life that may be holding you back. Convincing yourself that success is obtainable is the best thing you can do in getting it. You can read the books or listen to the tapes, but *if you don't believe you can have it, you won't.* Sorry to disappoint you, but no belief, no result.

By design, this book is here to help you get to the success that you want (or result). That's the first step in my program: Determining what it is that you desire. The second is giving you a little understanding along the way of why you may do the things you do and want the things you want. It may seem that we have missed step one, but believe me, we haven't. If you are reading this far, you my friend want to figure out what is holding you back from success or how to get more.

Fact is, my job in this process is simple. I'm here to help you determine *what you want and then give you the tools to install the* beliefs *so you can have it*. It's really less a matter of strategy than one of belief. You see, in these pages I've instilled the belief that love, understanding, success and honesty will become the driving forces in your life. Pretty tall order I know, but that's the truth. That's why you should understand the litmus test for truth.
Answer the following:

How do you know when something is true? Do you have to hear it, see it, or feel it?

For many, the answer encompasses a combination of the three. Even though we may see it and hear about it, unless we feel it, the event will remain distant to us. For most of us, unless the event is felt in some fashion, it won't be true to us. It's the "feeling" of success that the "gurus" out there forget to tell us about.

Many of the gurus provide the information, but not the answers. They give the steps, but not the reasons. It's the reasons for success that provide the feelings of success, though, and as I said before, it was the feeling of success that was missing in my life. At some level, I'm sure it is missing in yours as well.

Now that's a bold thing to assume, but I have a good idea of why you are reading these words at this moment. Something is missing in your life and you want to know a way to find it.

Maybe its money, a relationship, or an insight into what I may have to say that has brought you to this page. Perhaps you want to read something new or be exposed to a different way of thinking. You may be reading this book simply for entertainment.

What is "missing" from your life may not be clear to you, but your purpose in reading this book is. To fill the spot that is "missing" is what has brought you here. And "success" will be the result of whatever is missing. Filling a spot or getting an answer is a success.

If you discover one small technique or new way to look at things you will have success. Beyond these pages and into "real life" there are other examples of success. Say you've been single and you find someone: Success! The relationship you have, no matter the length, is a success. If you are "financially challenged" and become "financially secure", again you have success. When a child graduates to the next grade level? Success!

The examples of success are endless, but remember that when anything evolves from one state to another, the result is "success." All of these things have one simple element in common; a component becomes the rule for success.

This rule is carried out in everything you do, from the next breath you take to the next word you read. What is this rule for success? Simple.

Success = Life.

If you get nothing else from this book, you need to understand this one and only rule for success. I write rule, for that is what it is. All interpretations or lessons about success are the result of this rule. Success= Life. Life is success. Life is the process of success. Everything going around you is a "success." At our seminars, I like to compare success to a train.

Pulling the train is the steam engine or the *Rule of Success* (Success = Life). Each individual car is a *success lesson*.

Success Is Life
↓   Lesson↓

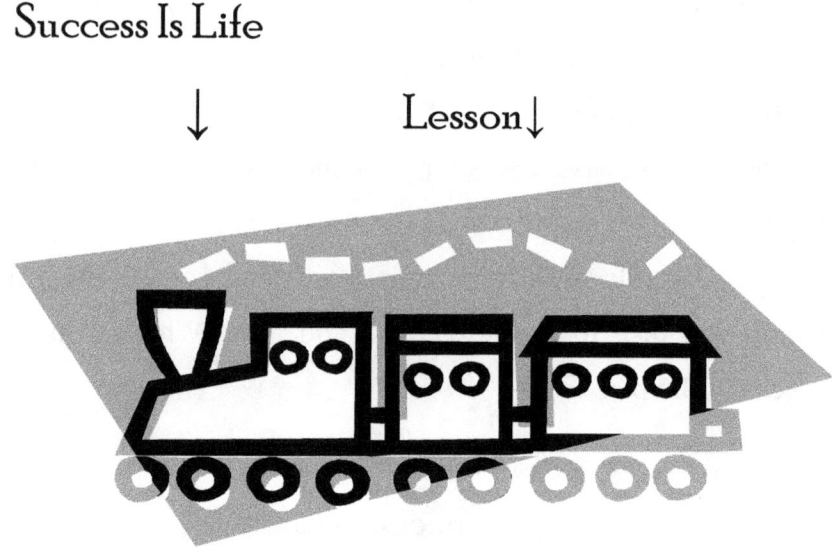

Have you ever watched a passing train and wondered, *"Is it ever going to end"*? I mean, have you ever seen a long train with a lot of cars attached to it? Well, success is the same way. There are hundreds, if not thousands, of ways to create a success train. There are numerous strategies, formulas, and get-rich-quick schemes that guarantee success. There are "life lessons" that you are taught or shown constantly, although many go unnoticed. But there is one important point that I'd like to share with you.

As with a "real train", the length of a train is of less importance to an engineer than weight distribution or where the heaviest cars are placed in the line of cars. Engineers know if you place the heaviest cars at the rear of the train, the train can de-rail at the first turn. That is why the heaviest cars are put towards the front of the line, closest to the steam engine. For a moment think of your life, and the way to get your own success, are like a train traveling the tracks of destiny, what should you do?

As the conductor and engineer of your own success train, you need to get the foundation cars hitched up to your engine in the beginning, instead of letting life put them at the end.

These "foundation cars" are your "success lessons." Let's begin by building yours now! How? By changing or at a minimum clarifying your beliefs and how they affect your life today.

Success lesson 1 - Changing Your Beliefs

What I took as my first lesson was that *to <u>feel success</u> I had too give it away with no strings attached.* Then I noticed that feelings followed the same path. For example, if I wanted love, I'd give it away …but ultimately end up feeling it. The same went for money: If I wanted more money, I'd give it away and it would in time come back to me. However, it wasn't the "material" result I was looking for, but the feeling associated with it. In technical terms, these feelings are *"neuro-associations."* In basic terms, they are *beliefs*.

Beliefs come from experience. I had to experience my friend telling me I was a "shallow jerk." By that occurrence I was able to see that I was on the wrong track. The belief that I had adapted wasn't delivering the results I wanted. <u>When I changed my belief, that's when my life changed.</u> The same can happen to you.

I'd like for you to think of something (a belief) that you hold true. It can something as simple as, a cliché, - like *it takes money to make money.*

Do you have your belief in mind? Then write it down. You can even use the edge of this page, I won't tell! Whatever that belief may be, I want to show you in the next chapters how it influences your success.

Kayton Kimberly

    One Belief I have is _____

    _____

Chapter 3

The 90% Club: A place for the Have-Nots

Every day it happens. People are grouped, classified and stereotyped into disturbing genres. Though the names have changed over the ages, this typecasting is nothing new. *Roughnecks* of the fifties have become the *bikers* of today, in a sense. *Queers* from days of old are now *gays* or five guys with a hit cable show. *Rappers* from the eighties are now called *"gangsters,"* although gangsters at one time were called *"mobsters."* If that's confusing enough, then there were the *geeks* who grew up to be *nerds*. The *nerds* open billion dollar companies and today are called the "Bill Gates" of the world. Amidst the names of yesterday and today you and I stand. Categorized by some socio-economic term, we're a statistic positioned between a class of higher and lower. There is no reason to fight or complain about it: Life and the great process of it perpetuate this evolution of sorts.

Some see it as *"climbing the ladder of success."* Others will say, *"They've fallen from grace."* One is always climbing while someone else is falling. It's the *ying to the yang*, the whole *"balance of life stuff"* we've heard a million times before. Yet, there are little known truths within all of that; tiny bits of honesty that we know in our hearts are real. Ask anyone who ever got the "starving kids in Africa" speech. The fact is we are always better off than someone else and worse off than others (even at the times we were forced to eat broccoli or believed that Santa would not visit our house). Luckily, things at their worst often times give way to better moments ahead.

Over time these thoughts have becomes clichés. As with *"One mans floor is another man's ceiling"* or *"To be the man you've got to beat the man,"* we reinforce our beliefs in our social standings. We convince ourselves that *"every cloud has a silver lining"* to help us get beyond the pain of failure. Even the founding fathers of the United States saw fit to say that *"all men are created equal,"* giving many the idea that no matter whom you are, you are no more superior than the man next you. Great philosophy, but we know it's not true.

We know that those of "privilege" have things afforded to them that many others don't. Everyone has seen the difference between great riches and great poverty. We know that better days may lie ahead, but in moments of despair, life can be painful. Ask anyone who has had their heart broken, lost a loved one, or failed a test. Somewhere inside all of our "titles" and positions and groups is the truth: that there are 2 groups of people. They are the Ninety per centers and the Tens.

Ninety per centers are the mass majority of people who do not have the success their life deserves. It sounds harsh, but that's the truth for the masses. Many will not take the time to think about what they want out of life and therefore won't get it. They will sit around waiting for things to happen. When things do happen, they will complain. Their life will be a matter of wishing, dreaming and doing nothing about their dreams. They will wait for the world to give them one opportunity or one great idea, and then let it passes on by. Many wish for six numbers to win the lottery or for quick-fix self-improvement pills, anything to create a better life. These are the people who make up the 90% club, a place for the have-not's.

Nine out of ten people have a chance of being in that club. The club doesn't care of what race, color or religion you are. It asks for no membership fees, and is open to everybody who is alive. From birth to death, you can be a 90 per center. You are born into a world that gives you success at each turn, but many of you will travel through this life unaware of how close you are to whatever it is that you desire. That is until now. Remember, Success = life. Success is life and success is a choice. That is all there is to it.

There is no need to clap your hands or recite things a hundred times into a mirror to feel success. You don't need some midnight infomercial guru to tell that success can be yours for three easy payments of $49.99. *To feel successful all that you need is the breath in your lungs and the thoughts of success.*

I find proving this point to be easy. Want to see for yourself? Really?

Take out a sheet of paper or at least think about the answer to this question. On a scale of 1 to 10 (with 10 being the highest), how would you score your current level of success? Where do you rate yourself? As a 5? Maybe even a 7?

What transpires in this exercise *and* in life is this: You were asked to rate your current success, to write a number that represents where you believe your success is now. Here is where it gets a little weird, for many are "wired" into thinking that their life is the best that it can be.

Many are led to believe that being "average" is okay. Some are taught that "greed is bad," or even that "success" takes a bunch of what they don't have. And most of the same people will refuse to take a simple test like the one you were just asked to do. They will say, *"I know where I stand, just tell me how to make more money."* I hear this all the time at my seminars. These people know that their lives are screwed up and they want a different answer that what I'm giving them. They miss the point, but by your reading this, I hope you won't.

In basic terms, the number you have chosen is a reflection of your current life. It's this "current life" that provides a sense of comfort. I always say, *"Be Wary of Being Comfortable".*

If there is any "comfort" in your current life, the chances of working past it are slim. Why? Two reasons.

One is that with comfort there is familiarity. We know what we have and are "okay" with it. It's like being in a "bad" relationship; you know it's bad, but why take a chance and perhaps get into one that is worse? The second is that it takes work to achieve goals (or success). Most have a curious view of work, and that view equates to the feeling that work isn't fun. Because it isn't fun, many of us won't do it.

What they're confusing is the idea of "work" in general with that of "success." That's because the resounding rule taught to many was that success takes *hard work* to obtain. No wonder there are so many Ninety per centers! Who wants to "work hard," much less work, period? Successful people do, that's who.

Successful people enjoy what they do. If they didn't, they wouldn't do it; it's that simple. This is a hard concept for most Ninety per centers to understand.

In the name of a "paycheck," many people do things that they don't want to do. Now, I know that in this modern day we all need an income to live, so what I am talking about is not our *"job"* but our *work*. There is a huge difference.

It looks like this –

Work = **what enhances our life**

Job = **what puts money in our pockets**.

Some may say they are one in the same, but I disagree. I've done plenty of things in my life for money, many of which I hated to do. The point is I didn't make a life out of doing *those* things. I didn't spend twenty years wishing for some type of security, social or otherwise. I decided to live my life, to live my work.

So if you want to get beyond being a Ninety per center, you will have to begin to look at things in a different light. You will have to give up some of some old ideas that you have had. And this change in perception begins with what "work" is.

Work can be defined as not only the effort of your actions towards a goal, but as a deeper gauge of your life. I believe it stands for **Words** that **Open Reality's Kitchen**. So what is *Reality's Kitchen?* Well, think of your own kitchen. What is in there? Maybe pots and pans, or oils and spices? Is your refrigerator full of food? How many recipe books are in the kitchen? Do you cook great meals or place your to-go boxes on the counter? Whatever the use, *inside your kitchen are the tools and ingredients to create meals that nourish you.* The combination of the right ingredients-, your thoughts and your actions-, brings you this thing called "work."

Success Side Note 5- *Work is what enhances your life while your job puts money in your pocket.*

What we do says a lot about who were are. *Reality's Kitchen* is a place inside of you where all of your thoughts and actions combine. This combination helps to create the *"job"* and work we pursue, as well as our feelings towards the same. If I were to ask you, "What do you do for a living?" you would tell me your job. Now if I were to ask you what the essence of your job is, could you answer?

Try it. Answer the following question- *What is the essence of what I do? (Describe your job in 3 words)*

_____

_____

_____

What words do you use on a consistent basis to describe what you do? Are these words the result of you being happy at your job? Let's look at it from another perspective.

Ask any kid what they want to be when they grow up. They will tell you with feeling and conviction that being a doctor or a pro-athlete is what they want to do. You can even get a kid who hates to write to create a good essay on *"what they want to be when they grow up."* Their "kitchen," however compact and limited with experience, is full of reasons "why."

For example, look at the "successes" of today who were prodigies in their fields. *Michael Jackson* danced since he could walk.

Tiger Woods hit golf balls before the age of four. *Britney Spears* sang her butt off as a child. I'm sure none of them "hate" their jobs or do it for the money alone. In their kitchens, they cooked up wanting to be great "performers" (yes, golf can be a *performance* at times). Those who are "successes" and those who aren't yet are no different; it's what's in their *Reality's Kitchen* that makes the difference.

Tony Robbins once told me, *"Who you spend time with you will become."* This relates not to just the people in your life but to you as well. You spend most of your time with *"you."* With that in mind you had better start speaking well of yourself. If you don't, no one else will.

Realize that when we get to our job, we have to deal with other people. The people we associate with at particular employers, our co-workers and competitors, all speak the same "language." After all, vocations have their own lingo. Real estate agents talk about real estate. Foot doctors talk about feet. If you spend any amount of time with a group of like-minded people and utilize the same words, your "reality" will become exactly that, good or bad, positive or negative. Anyway, let's try a brief exercise to prove my point.

Do you know some-one who seems to get the "short end of the stick" always? A person who is always trying to do things but nothing happens? Well, if you could imagine how they would "score" their success on the 1 to 10 scale, what do you think it would be?

Imagine that you are in *their* shoes for a moment. What you would say if I asked you what went "wrong" with all of those things that were attempted? Could you tell me *the* reasons why the things didn't work out? Would there be many excuses, like "well, such- and- such screwed me out of a deal," or "the rates went up," or "the bank wouldn't finance me"? (Remember, I'm asking you to look at *someone else's life*, not yours.)

Take a moment to fill in the blanks below with a few of your notations. Remember to fill in *"their* score" first, then the reasons why things went wrong for them, not you.

Score_____

Reasons why things "**Don't** work out"

(List at least 3 excuses for things not working out)

Next, I'd like you to take a moment and think about someone whom you consider to be "successful." This person would be a 10 on the scale, or at the least, a high 9. Do you know somebody like this?

What I'd like you to do now is imagine being *them* for a moment. Imagine having of all of the great things that *they* have in your life. Bring the pictures of their success into your mind. Think about all the great things they do. Can you imagine your life like that? Now imagine how they accomplished the various successes in their life. If you were to ask them, how they achieved so much, what do you believe their answers would be? How confident would you be in any advice they were giving? If you were face- to - face with a "successful" person, would you hear excuses or the confidence that success has brought to them?

Take a moment to fill the following blank in with a score of a 10. Then capture a few of the reasons a "success" might say that things <u>have worked out</u> for them.

Kayton Kimberly

Score___ (9-10)____

Reasons why things
Did "work out"

Remember, I asked you to *imagine* what life is like on "both sides." I asked you to correlate a "score" to what many feel is "success" and to what can be considered "failure." Did you do the exercise? What were some of the things you wrote down for getting this thing called success? What about "failure;" did you write down some good "excuses"? Putting such things down on paper can move you from a place of failure and frustration to a place of success and freedom within a few moments. This should help you to see the power that is possible within each of us.

Now let's look at your life for a moment. Of the two people you were asked to imagine, whom do you score closer to, the one "unsuccessful" person or the *image of success*? Or are you half way between the two? Is your life a reflection of what you had placed down as less than a "success"? If your answer is yes, then don't worry.

There are infinite ways to find success. Within this infinite realm of possibilities stand you. Where you stand (or sit) right now was the result of a decision. Each decision you have made over your lifetime has brought with it a related action. From the food you eat to the person you asked to the prom, each little thing has helped create your life. Even reading this far has had influenced some part of your existence.

This influence extends into your level of success as well, for both the short- term and the long- term. The reason for this is that your mind doesn't know the difference between what is "real" and what is imagined. *If you believe that you already possess* what *ever it is you want your mind will focus on that success.* That focal point will then come to fruition. And this isn't motivational speaking, but real life.

"Real life" is what many 90 per centers miss. They miss it not for lack of opportunity or knowledge, but for a lack of focus. You need to focus on what you want and what life can give you. Focus on the things that matter to you.

Success Side Note 6 – *What matters most to you is a reflection of things you picked up along the way through life- beliefs can change.*

How many times in your life do you examine what matters most to you? For many, it is once a year, around January first. Others do so when it comes to a birthday then ends with a "zero." Then there are those who wait on a tragedy to remind them that life is precious. For most the knowledge or change brought about by these events doesn't last. And what many fail to realize is *that in each moment the gifts that bestow the things you want are given.* The secret is that *it is up to you to decide what those things are.*

There is no great mystery to success. The answers are simple. Look to the rule of success: Life = success, Success=life. Success is a reflection of life. And in the previous exercises, you have been exposed to a fact that many don't give a second thought: that *reality is based upon perceptions*. Here is way to test this.

If you considered yourself a 7, is your life reflecting that? Are your friends what you would call 7's as well? Take a moment to notice if your life is indeed a reflection of what your current "score" is. Now take it to the next level. Put this book down, walk outside (if you are able and not flying, driving, confined to a prison cell, if so then it's ok to imagine) and take a good look at your surroundings. Are there visible signs of what you consider your life to be? Look at the cars, the housing, and the people in general whom you live around and spend time with, and then come back to this point.

My experience from sharing this exercise is that most times people respond, "Yes."

At this point I believe I have made my point. Yet sometimes another argument arises. Many people challenge whether they should work any harder, change any thing in their lives, because they feel being a 7 (or a 6 or a 5) is not so bad." Well, if it's not so bad, *then why are you reading this book?*

Think about this. How different would your life be if you felt it was a 5 and then it became a 9? Would you have more or less? As a 5, you might perceive your life as enjoyable, but more challenging. As a 9, you would see your life as "almost successful." For many, being a 9 could mean an "easier life."

Yet this is all an exercise in perception. *Your life is based on the way you are seeing things.* For it is from perceptions that feelings are created.

When I am speaking to groups often I will have everyone change seats partway through my program. The reason is that I want each person to get a different perspective on what is being taught. Another benefit (for me) is being able to watch people get "frustrated" or angry that someone is "taking their chair." It helps to break up the "learning" experience and because of these actions and reactions, participants are experiencing feelings.

When you did the exercise in this chapter there were a few things that transpired. One is that you had to go inside yourself. You had to change your focus, and create reasons for things "working out" as well as excuses for things "not working out." All of this leads us back to what you had designated as your original "score." What I'm saying is that, *if it was anything other than a 10, go back and change it*. Put a little mark through it and make it a 10. This task is a simple yet profound one, for within that one and that zero is the genesis of your success.

With changing your old score to a 10, you will have begun a journey that will take you beyond your current limitations. The journey will start with you feeling different in the way you feel about yourself, your surroundings, and perhaps even those whom you have come to call your friends as well. I can't say if your feelings will be stronger or weaker; the intensity of them will be based on how far you want to go and how determined you are to change. You may like your current life and just want to expand its horizons a bit and that's fine. All I am speaking of here is perspective, or the way you see things.

Yet change as we know can create new challenges. Not comfort. Whenever we move beyond our comfort zones, we are faced with a host of new ideas. I've had people in seminars start to freak out when they hear they should change their number from a 5 to a 10. They've lived their lives for such a long time with such a certain identity that, anything else is uncomfortable for them. In such cases, I suggest baby steps as a solution. Maybe instead of going straight for the 10, simply go up a point or two and that's it.

All of this uneasiness is natural. You see, uncertainty for most doesn't feel good, and in admitting on paper that you can be something more by just writing down a number, forces a decision. It means you are making a choice to move forward. That shift beyond your comfort zone may not "feel" good. The same holds true when it comes to changing any limiting behavior, such as a bad habits or compulsions.

More often than not, breaking the "habits" that we call "bad" boils down to feeling one thing and *it's not that you can't change*, but *that you may feel like you aren't comfortable making the change*. In others words, you think there may be pain or loss as a result of the changing process.

Well you can erase this feeling of doubt by looking back at the exercise and noticing what you wrote for the "10 person." For that exercise you wrote down compelling reasons why a person has "success." By doing the exercise, you had to "feel" success on some level (even if was was all imagined) and that is how you were able to write the answers down on paper. Your perception of success (real or not) has given you a reference point from which to work. Remember that to be successful, *success first needs to be felt inside*. And the reality is that inside; you have what it takes to be a 10.

The greatest part of this is that *this is where your success begins.* By starting here you have the same chance of success as does anyone else. It doesn't guarantee it, but now you are among 90% of the population that can succeed. Take a moment to be proud: you made into the club. But don't relish in your happiness too for long.

The club isn't an exclusive guild, and the membership requirements do seem to be lacking sometimes, I mean look at some of the people you know who are in the same club. There's the girl down the hall whose cat won't stop meowing, your annoying in-laws who stay much longer than they need to, and the rude check-out person at the grocery store. It would almost seem that everyone you know is a member of this club, but heck, you're happy right?

I am willing to bet that you are not happy, that you may not be feeling successful right now. I know I felt that way for years. I felt that I was just living instead of being alive. I had the same type of friends you may have at present and the same crappy jobs we all hated. I had my share of frustrations and more than enough of my share of tragedy in my life.

But I have also enjoyed a bounty of happy moments as well, and I am sure this is true in your life also. There is a mixture of "sun and clouds" in each of our lives. I say all of this for *success is life,* but there is a difference between success and being successful. *The journey from success to being successful begins in four letters and they are I.D.E.A.* That stands for **Internal Desires Expressed Alone**.

Success is an individual idea. You can be successful to others and feel terrible inside. Or you can be dead broke and happy. <u>Being successful starts with the thoughts that you alone come up with.</u> And it all goes back to perception. That is why I asked you to replace your old score with a 10. At the time, it may have seemed like a simple request, but now can you see that by changing your self-perception you have begun to change yourself. This change is happening even though you may not realize it. To show how simple this truth is, I'd like you to do the following exercise and experience success:

Success = Freedom Exercise

Since we have established that success=life, we must create a universal rule that can define "success." For the sake of argument, let us agree that success is the freedom to do what you want whenever you want. With that in mind, I would like you *to feel happy right now!* That's right, go on and feel happy. No one is looking. Put that smile on your face Laugh if you like.

Now what does being happy feel like? Can you describe it?

*****

Next, I would like you *to feel angry!* Get mad. Get a little pissed off. If you need some help with this, then think of the person who cut you off in traffic the other day or the person at work who steals your ideas. Are you feeling the slight bit angry yet? Can you think of a few other things that get you mad? Good. Stay this way for at least 30 seconds.

******

Okay, clear your mind, take a deep breath and relax for a minute before you get back to reading. Return to the curious state that you were in before I asked you just now to *experience success*! That's right! (I wrote that you **experienced success** because you just did!)

By doing this *happy-angry exercise* you exercised the "freedom" to do what you want when you want equaling "success" in your life. By the fact of you simply being alive, *success is yours*. Tony Robbins once told me as well, *"Nothing in life has any meaning except the meaning you give it."* The meaning to this exercise was to show you how a feeling (be it happy or angry) correlates to life (you have to be alive to feel things) and how we attach "success" to experiencing that feeling. You may have a different belief in what success is than the next person, but this is meant to get you headed in the direction of success.

Many ninety per centers just go along missing the meaning of things. However, that's not what these exercises or book is about. The book is titled *Repossess Your Life* for a reason. This book, and these exercises, has been delivered to your hands as a way to help you think on a conscious level. And being aware of things is the first step.

The exercise that asked you to change your score from a _ to a 10 was done by thinking. That new philosophy placed you on the path to success. But positioning isn't enough to complete the journey. *To get the success you want, you will need to find your own I.D.E.A.* You can do that by answering a simple yet profound question:

What is success to me?

Take a few quiet moments to answer the question. Forget what your neighbors or family think; answer the question, *what is success **to me?*** You can answer it by looking inside. It is inside of you where change takes place. Each change, no matter how large or small in your life, is a spark calling you to action. And it's with the actions you take that your life begins to transform.

To move from things that have held you back begins as an I.D.E.A. Taking that passion and moving forward then becomes your torch. Acting upon your thoughts, whims and desires will lead you from the barren cave walls of the 90% club. Escaping mediocrity leads to the exclusive club called the 10% Resort. It is there where life begins to be lived at a whole new level.

In the 10% Resort you get to look across the abyss to see the shadow of your past life being whisked away by the breeze of yesterday. That is the place you will go, if you want to, by reading further and doing the exercises. Success, true success, is lived by people who first get honest and decide to do something about it.

Often when I am coaching a group I will ask, "How many of you in fact want to be here?" The answers are for the most part unanimous; they all *want* to be there. Then I'll ask, "If your boss or supervisor wasn't here, how many of you would rather be at the beach?" I get a few giggles but the fact is almost no-one will be honest enough to raise their hand. To this day, it still blows my mind how many people aren't honest with themselves or others. But as we know, there are explanations for things such as this.

Look at some of the ideas distilled into us. Sayings like, "Don't rock the boat" or "Don't challenge authority" are common messages that are taught. We are told to be honest with others, to not tell lies. Yet in our attempts to be courteous we end up lying to ourselves. With these soft truths or "white lies" we become charter members of the 90 percent club, often for a lifetime. We forget what success is or never ask ourselves what we want on our terms. Now is the time to change that. Are you going to "get busy living, or get busy dying," as in the powerful movie *The Shawshank Redemption* Are you going to rise to the challenge of creating a better life?

Success Side Note 7- *Decision is a choice. Success is a choice.*

And deciding to be a success is the way to "live." Ignoring the possibility of success, or pretending that you will never have success is a way to "die." People like this seem as if they are dead inside. As each day comes, they dread getting out of bed. Their whole life is a statement of "What's the use?" They get busy dying. Ignoring the opportunities around them, they live out their days working for a living and never living their work. Many give up before ever getting started. *Don't make the same mistake. Don't ignore what can be.*

Things happen in life. Right now there are billions of actions and reactions happening around the world. In the time you are taking to read this, think of all the births, deaths, divorces and marriages that are occurring. Right now someone became a millionaire and someone else lost it all. Life happens. <u>If you want real success, you must master the skill set of thinking on a consistent basis of what it is you want and less of what you don't want.</u>

One way to accomplish this is by making yourself a reminder sign and placing in where you will see it the most. It should read as follows- <u>*Am I concocting stuff to do to avoid the Important*</u>

Joining the 10% Resort takes effort and it takes thought, but all the labors will be worth their experience. These understandings come as the result of working towards your success. Working in the sense of not only actions but understanding the thoughts you have towards your work as well.

Success= Thinking Your Way towards It + The time between now and then + The actions you take.

You have to *think* instead of just *"do."* In the beginning this is a challenge for many 90 per centers. For too long they have survived in "auto pilot," numb to the world they desire. Most respond to things instead of creating them. And that is where you will have to be different.

Thinking on the "successful level" is a two- part equation. It can be expressed as follows.

- Step 1- Seeing challenges (or problems) for what they are and as they are.
- Step 2 – Seeing how to utilize those challenges *for your benefit.*

If you can master those two steps, you can become a Ten. By having a different way of "doing" things you then can move into the resort. There aren't many Tens who have made it any other way. A simple fact to remember is that the 90 per center's *desire success* and the Tens *are success*. The difference is one wants, and one has. Which do you want to be? Well look at the reality of your life before you answer that question.

Success comes from action, and not excuses, but Ninety per centers make excuses; the Tens of the world make things happen. One of the greatest excuses we use is "I Wish."

An excuse like "I wish" is nothing more than a *wanting* for change, rather a *doing*. "I wish I were rich," "I wish I were pretty," or any other thing we on occasion whisper to ourselves can destroy everything that may have accomplished up to that point. It's almost like starting over again and again.

We can get within inches of success and then scare it away by saying, "I wish." Another excuse it is to end a sentence with "but." Here's an example:

"I would love to make a million dollars, but…" or "I'd love to lose weight, but…"

If you want freedom, it begins with writing down what you want. That is it. It doesn't have to be a huge gigantic goal like "saving the world" but something as simple as "help one person." How? We'll cover solutions later in this book, but for now, here are some answers. You can give them this book, or you can make a meal for a homeless person. You can help yourself by committing to act on your impulses. Whatever is right for you, *capture it*.

With each moment you can desire to be a success or you can *be* a success; the choice is yours. The choice has always been yours, so decide now to become a success and then come along with me to a place where few reside, but many wish to.

Where 10 is not a mere number, but something more substantial, it is a way of thinking, doing and obtaining. A place where I believe success is automatic.

Chapter 4

The other 10% (And a Virtual Tour of the Resort)

A tropical breeze stirs the salty smell of crystal blue waters. On the beach, a cabana boy with a reddish-colored drink in hand walks feverishly towards you. In your hand you hold a crisp *$100.00*. The tiny pink paper umbrella in dances atop a sea of ice as you trade a *Benjamin* for a *Bacardi*. He walks away smiling as you think to yourself, *"winter in the tropics..., what's a millionaire to do?"* Your mind travels. *"Maybe I'll have Robin Leach over for crumpets and tea later?"* Your mind wanders over the vastness that is *your* success. Isn't life great?

But wait a minute. Things aren't as they seem. That tropical breeze is no breeze at all; it's the a/c vent over your cubicle. The smell of the crystal blue waters is "Dave" from accounting wearing his *hi karate* aftershave. You may be so lucky as to have the guy in shipping bring you an envelope, but no one is bringing you a drink today. And the only tip you'll give is about some crappy stock that no one wants or in a speech to your kids. Being a ninety per center sucks! Life just doesn't seem fair… and that's your reality.

The truth of your success is that there is no tropical beach. There is no lunch with Leach. A daily grind and the desire to get out are the menu items for today. You read the books, you listened to the tapes and yet you still sit there, looking for "success." You notice others in the office and wonder how their lives seem to be successful and wonder why? Why don't I have the success my life deserves? You go home and watch another infomercial on how to get this illusive thing called "success." Your mind creates endless answers to endless questions. It rationalizes everything from your childhood to the thousands of other excuses why your life doesn't work.

You get caught up for the moment in how unfair life seems to be until it's interrupted by some other illusion. It's a chimera of something that does nothing for your "success." Things like "housework" or a "to-do" list are what will capture your attention, erasing your thoughts of dreaming about what you want (although you won't realize it).

The next day you return to your grind or what many call a "job." Your illusion of hope returns disguised as success. Hidden beneath that pile of paperwork is your "success." It comes with the old idea of *"work hard and get ahead in life."* You can't remember where you heard it, but right now it seems to be the right answer. It's a solution that utters, *"Reaching your success means working harder,"* and so you do. You toil away at the empty promise of doing "good work" and getting "good rewards." Then it happens all over again.

After a few hours or days or even weeks, you find yourself leaning back in 8- by- 8 prison cell you call your office. Daydreams about a wonderful life and the visions of a sandy beach far, far away return. You think to yourself, *"God if I had more money, more time, more looks, more of whatever everybody else has, then my life would be great" "I could then do all of the things I want to do."*

Does any of this sound familiar? Have you done this at least once in your life? Well it's called the <u>Cycle of Mediocrity</u>, and it's a cycle that continues for every nine out of ten people.

So who can break this cycle? This self- imposed prison of weakness? You may be asking yourself on some level "If life is success, why am I still dreaming about a beach instead of reading this on the beach?" The answer to all of these questions and more reside at a place called the 10% Resort.

This is where the successes of life reside, the top 10% of anything. This is the place reserved for those people and it's where all 90 per centers desire to get but few will.

However by making your current I.D.E.A about success a 10, you have opened the gates to the resort, a place where life is played at a new level, and enjoyed to its fullest. As you enter the gates of the 10% Resort, there are a few things you need to become aware of.

Many who tour the "other side" have a difficult time returning to the 90% club. For once they have become exposed to the possibility of what success can bring to their lives; they continue on to become a Ten. They see what success is like, and dismiss all of the old dogmas that have held them back. If you are the least bit curious about seeing the 10% Resort, then I need for you to answer these questions.

- Is this something that you can do?
- Can you get honest?
- Can you find an I.D.E.A.?
- Are you a 10 (Ten) on paper? How about in your mind?

Success Side Note 8- *Tens get "success" by first deciding to be successful.*

Do you still want to see life at the resort? I am going to pretend that you said "yes" to all the preceding questions, and with that in mind, invite you along as the tour begins. (Please make sure your seats are in the upright position and your tray tables are put away.)

"This is your Captain speaking. Looking out the starboard window, we can see the 10% Resort. We will be landing in 10 minutes"...

There is a place that all of those who obtain their success reside, and although it exists around the world, we may never see an advertisement or map showing its exact location.

Some have written about similar places throughout time, places like *Babylon, Camelot* and *Atlantis,* but these were simply attempts to camouflage the *real* location of the Resort. Why the mystery?

There are some who may argue not all are deserving of joining the ranks of the Tens. These people feel success is reserved for them, and they attempt to discourage any discussion on accepting new members. It is the people who do not understand the responsibility that success brings. By denying others access to the resort, they deny themselves from the very success that has placed them there. As luck will have it, this is but a small percentage of the Tens.

It is a small group, though, that is easy to recognize. Its members are the ones that complain about everything be it the neighborhood or in government, yet do nothing about it. They are the same people at work who attempt to keep others down by ignoring requests for assistance and taking credit for others' actions. Well they may be part of the Tens, but they are not the majority. The small percentages of people who have gained success at the expense of others are no better off than the ninety per centers they used to be. *The success they will have will be limited*; it will not last. This minority is not the majority at the 10% Resort.

Over time this has become a challenging concept to understand and accept. Many believe that success immediately changes people into "untouchable" or complaining troublemakers, and they give them nicknames like "snob" or "condo commando." Others call them "county commissioners" or "politicians." Understand that in every society, from those who are considered "poor" to the "wealthy," there will always be a small percentage of people whose job in life is to aggravate everyone else. They are placed here to remind us of what we don't want to be like.

Here are a few other points to make mental notes of.

Success will magnify an individual's I.D.E.A. If their internal desire is to complain, then being successful will provide them with more to complain about. If someone's desire is to help others, then success will give those more to help others with. To illustrate these two points, look at Fidel Castro and Mother Teresa.

Exiling himself from the rest of the world, Castro is seldom heard from. When he does speak, all he does is whine about how poor his country is. He does nothing to improve the lives of his countrymen thus the "success" he has created is limited. On the other hand, Mother Teresa was renowned the world over for her caring. Upon her passing, world dignitaries came to pay respects and the streets were lined with thousands of people. Success gave her the ability to help thousands of people and remind the world of what the power of the human spirit is about. These two are a small fraction of the millions of Tens around the world.

So where *is* this resort, you may be ask. The resort is anywhere in the world we find a Ten. Its walls are not made of gold and its streets lined with chocolate. No, this resort is inside the thoughts and actions of everyone who has obtained success. It has been said that, "success leaves clues." The real answer is that Tens leave clues, and other Tens recognize them. That is how the resort can be found anyplace you find a Ten. And the simple truth is that everybody is a Ten, although most don't realize it.

The truth is that life provides success. Each moment in time is an opportunity to turn any dream into a reality. Think of all the stories of people "just like you" who tried something and "failed," only for there to be another person who comes along and does the same thing and "succeeds." Is that fair? The answer to that is ahead, but first become aware of a few other points about the Resort.

It is a co-operative, which means that everyone has a stake in its growth and expansion. Members own their shares of the resort, and will not trade them with any ninety per centers (for in fact, as you know, many Tens were once like yourself, so why go back?) However, ownership is open to anyone and the 10% Resort welcomes all who wish to join.

Other facts about Tens are that many find that they enjoy spending more time at the resort with others such as themselves. It is not meant to be a social club, but as humans we tend to like people who are like ourselves (a fact you can test by looking at your current group of friends). Are you surrounded by Tens or are they members of the 90 percent club? How many of your current friends would buy the idea that *they* could be a Ten simply by getting honest with themselves? When you get the success you want, will you have many of these same "friends"? These are a few things to consider as your tour proceeds.

Moving onto some of the benefits of membership, becoming a member of the 10% Resort provides many with the freedoms to travel where and by any means they wish. It is this idea of freedom that lures many to seek success and yet few seem to find what is already available by being alive. They tell themselves, "When I become rich, I will travel the world." The truth is the "freedom to do what you want," is an I.D.E.A. A person is as "free" as their thoughts; however, the Tens have a way of taking an idea and expanding upon it. It is by doing this that many become members at the 10% Resort.

When asked, many members suggest that getting *lost* (that's L.O.S.T.) is what brought them here to the resort. L.O.S.T. is understood as **Living on Silenced Thoughts.** It is different from an I.D.E.A., and is what separates the 90 per centers from the Tens. If you can do this, you are almost guaranteed placement in the resort.

Success Side Note 9 - *Getting lost isn't So Bad after All-Living on Silenced Thoughts*

Take a deep breath and go back in time for a moment. Remember when you were a ninety per center? Remember all the *ideas* you had about success? All of the times you expressed them out loud to your friends and family and all they did was tell you how your *ideas* were foolish? They would tell you to stop dreaming, as only "successful people" could do those things? Well it is true, the successful (the Tens) do those things, whatever they may be. How? By Living On the Silenced Thoughts. That is what *getting "LOST" in your thoughts (or ideas)* is about.

Those who have successful lives stop dreaming and start living. They (Tens) took their ideas (or somebody else's) and made them work. Many would not quit even when many 90 per centers told them to. Tens do not live by the advice of others unless it comes from a source that has done what they desire to do. In other words Tens don't give up.

If they don't like the answers they are getting, they either ask better questions or seek the knowledge of those who believe in what they have to say. It's like asking your mechanic about tax lien certificates or the stock market: Even if they have had success in those areas, it is not their specialty! That's the difference between a Martin Luther King and some kid in the third grade that you don't remember. That's the difference between the pyramids in Egypt and some sand castle on the beach. In each of the cases Tens take IDEAS and create the visible equivalents.

The call for equal rights in America was a long battle that began from the days when the first slaves were placed on the soil of the United States. It was not a new "idea" that Dr. Martin Luther King Jr. expressed, but he made it a reality by living on the silent thoughts of many before him. The pyramids in Egypt are still standing today as a testament to the desire for immortality. The idea there was to create palaces for royalty so that they could live on in the lifestyle befitting them after they had passed on. As obvious as these two examples are, the reality is that both Dr. Martin Luther King Jr. and the great engineers who created the pyramids finished what many had begun before them. Yet King and the engineers of the pyramids were Tens who got *lost* and ended up at the Resort.

As we wind down our tour of the Resort there is one other thing, perhaps the most important point of all. *Once you become a Ten, you can never go back to being a ninety per center.* Once you are "successful" you then own the tools for re-gaining that success, no matter how many times it may take. If you make a fortune and lose it all, don't worry you, will make a come back. If your marriage fails, have no fear, the days of loneliness will be overshadowed by the new love that you will find. Tens know this and live by this fact everyday. They *know that there are no failures in life but that there are results.*

This "knowledge" in being a Ten comes from the fact that as a 90 per center, you have the right to success but it is limited. That restriction is based upon there being many affiliate members. You see there are a lot of 90 per centers in the world so you will have to share your "rights to success with them." On the other side, as a Ten, you own your share, so there is nothing to divide among the other owners. You get to keep your success and watch it grow.

That is about it. I hope you enjoyed the virtual tour of the 10% Resort. If you still have any doubts about those who are Tens then look at this short list of owners. See if you recognize any names.

Thomas Edison, Ben Franklin, Michael Jordan, Anthony Robbins, Steve G Jones, Robert Allen, Hulk Hogan, Jim Carrey, Jerry Bruckheimer, John F. Kennedy, Bill Clinton, Ray Croc, Susan B. Anthony, Bill Gates, The Tampa Bay Buccaneers Football Team, Bubba The Love Sponge, Dick Clark, Chris "Kanyon" Klucsartis, Wayne Weaver, Kayton Kimberly, John Maxwell, Dr. Robert Schuller, Robert Kiyosaki , Claudia Holton, The Detroit Red-Wings, Vic Conant, T Harv Eker, Dale, Jackie, Danielle, Kristine, Brad and Karen (you know who you are) And the list goes on.....

With the "tour" complete, let us get back to grasping the concept of the 10% Resort.

Success Side Note 10- <u>10% more Adds Up to a Lost-it is the difference between of success and the successful.</u>

The difference between having success and being successful is done by applying 10% to whatever one desires. As my old football coach would tell me, "It's taking the ball the last ten feet and scoring." Here are some examples of what I mean.

Want to be rich? Save 10% of your paycheck every week for 20 years (do the math; it is not that much per week). Want to be an excellent lover? Last 10% longer in bed (the average male *lasts* 15 minutes, so only 1.5 minutes would be needed). Want to be a great ball player? Then hit 10% more balls. Want to write a book? It's easy enough to find the time. Take 10% of the time you would otherwise waste by watching TV (an average of 17 hours per week times 10%, thus giving you 1 hour and 42 minutes a week) to create your masterpiece.

Those who have successful lives do what they want to do and *devote 10% more time to it every day of their lives.* They get that "extra" time by knowing that this thing called success is not that difficult to obtain. By being alive they are 90% there and any rewards that are received come from the other 10% that they apply.

Successful people also know the Rule for Success (**Success = Life**). Many describe success as being at the end of a hundred foot length. The prize (success) is in a bowl at the end of the 100 feet. Life gives them an advance to the 90-foot mark. The last ten feet is up to them.

Note that the rewards and the 100 foot length are all *self imposed*. That's the *real secret* most gurus forget to tell you! As mentioned earlier, it is up to the individual as to how they want to pursue the last ten feet. For just as each person carries within an idea of what "success" is, they too also can be burdened with needless ways to gain that desired reward, for *unless a person creates mountains then there are no mountains to climb.*

Yet for every way to do something there are references that can help make the process easier. What I'm talking about here are *strategies*. Ways in which those who have gained success have accomplished whatever it is you desire.

Success is not a mystical thing that many don't ever experience. Often, though, people forget to, or haven't been taught to, ask for what they want. Many can't recognize that success is granted to them in each breath they take or in nature. And it's in the nature that surrounds us that success can be copied. We can see the purpose of success in a thing such as tree.

A tree doesn't sit around and say, "I guess I want to grow." A tree grows and then it dies. The *success* a tree has *is in its lifetime*, no matter how long or short that may be. If it never makes out of the ground as a seedling, it will provide nourishment to the soil. On the other hand, if it is to grow for a hundred years or more, it will provide numerous benefits to the world: shelters for small animals, moving the winds, creating oxygen, and so on. Again, success comes from life. Success *is* life itself. A tree grows and dies: that is its purpose. It can't ask for anything else.

We grow and we die as well, but during that time <u>we can ask of the world around us what we want from it.</u>

Thousands of years ago, a caveman asked, "How can I get warm?" and discovered that a tree could give him this magical thing called fire. Hundreds of years ago, many asked, "Is there a place where we can worship freely?" and discovered that by taking a chance of sailing the seas, a new land was found and a new country full of religious freedom was formed.

Think of your own life. Over the past 5 years, can you remember some of the things you asked for and received? It could be time again to ask out of life what it is that you want. Maybe you'll ask that it'll be time for you to become a Ten? To live the rest of your days at the Resort that was made for *you*.

Such success can be yours, it already is. You don't have to be smart, lucky or born with silver –spoon. All you have to be is *alive.*

Look no further than the last ten feet of this hundred-foot mark called "success." Success isn't this huge massive thing, *life is,* and you are here to tell about it. That's what the ownership rights of success are about. *You have to ask of life what your purpose is, instead of having life create a purpose for you.* It is your *right* to ask. Many don't, for they weren't taught or are unsure as to how. But all you have to do is to get honest and decide what you want your life to be about. From this purpose you will find the path to walk down for your success.

Success Side Note 11- *Don't Walk the Path to Success All by Yourself*

However, success is not a path for you to travel alone. Over time, many have traveled the same path (the last ten feet) as others who have claimed the same rewards. This is called "modeling." Still others have made their own path and created the rewards that were due to them. Success (life) provides a way for the Tens of the world to decide which path to follow. These paths aren't stringent. There are no major penalties for copying the success of others. In fact, if you do the same things, you would get the same results so dare to copy someone else; it's ok. No one will care except for you.

Remember that *the difference between being a success and being successful is 10%.* Utilizing 10% more of your passion and resources will bring you the success you desire and deserve. Again think back to the examples I cited earlier. Dr. Martin Luther King brought to the forefront what many others had done through out time. He was not the first man to "stand up" for what he believed in, nor will he be the last. He didn't invent the idea of equal rights. What he did was to live out the desires of others. He accomplished this by protesting the unequal treatment of Afro-Americans. The results he obtained came from looking at others. Utilizing a spirit of change, be it from Jesus or Gandhi, he made a difference.

By modeling the success of others Dr. King's life became an example. A paradigm in the way we see each other. You too can utilize the same power.

Yes, you have the option of figuring it out on your own. As most know, this then becomes a process of "trial and error." A way to learn what works and what doesn't in the drive towards success. Either way it is up to the individual as to how they want to proceed.

And through it all of this remains the one constant: *Success = life*. Whatever the case, success results from passion. You can tap into that passion which has been missing or never discovered. You can find that extra 10% that makes all the difference. All you have to do is ask.

One of the best ways I have found to get that extra 10% of passion is leverage. It's a resource for that provides a genesis for success. Leverage comes from utilizing the talents of others to help you achieve your goals. When others believe in what you want to accomplish, they will help you. This synergy creates passion for all to move forward and to achieve the success that is desired. All the great successes in the world have used leverage throughout time.

Think about this. When was the last time you saw Donald Trump mowing his lawn? Never. Why? He makes more money doing real estate deals than he does mowing his own lawn. He leverages the time and talents of others so he can concentrate on what he wants to do. And what he wants to do is his passion. From this he surrounds himself with others who enjoy the same idea. That's leverage at work. Starting in a place of passion and by leverage Mr. Trump creates success in his life.

Another example is Bill Gates. Have you ever seen him on the assembly line making software or writing code? Hell no, that's what he has employees for. Bill Gates passion is to have a program that all computers will utilize. He can't do that by taking out the trash or signing 2,000 paychecks. Doing such would only detract him from his goal. Anyone who is successful knows that leverage is the key, the means to creating lasting success. Leverage though has one other important factor. That feature is its effect on time. There are twenty-four hours in day. And that becomes the great equalizer among each of us.

We all <u>do not</u> have the same background, education or same resources. <u>What is equal, however, is the time we have.</u> *Leveraging provides the power to utilize as many resources as we can in the limited time we are given.* It is the way to have the small efforts of many combine into huge results. That becomes part of the responsibility of success. *The more people you can leverage, the more your success is shared and then grows.* We can see examples of this throughout the world.

For instance, there are the seven wonders of the planet including the *Sphinx, the Great Wall of China*, and *the Pyramids in Egypt*. Beyond those, we live in a modern world with *Disney-land, Coca-Cola, Outback Restaurants,* and *automobiles*. All of this and more results from leveraging. Utilizing people's time, efforts and ideas has brought us most of what we see. Throughout time this is how success shows itself, as a way to bring something that becomes visible to all.

Someone sat around and thought, "Hey I'd like a place that serves great food" or "I'd like to take that person out on a date." Those thoughts are an *internal desire expressed alone*. What happened next is that the idea person got L.O.S.T. Their idea became so strong that it became what they "lived" for.

From the examples above, let's use *Outback* Restaurants. With *Outback*, a single establishment was opened in Tampa, Florida. That was the *idea*. When that happened, the owners decided then to get *lost*. Many before them, from *Colonel Sanders* to *Ray Croc*, had done what they now set out to do. But there were also countless others who didn't. The difference was that the owners of *Outback lived on* those *silenced thoughts,* which lead them to open several locations around the world (over 19 countries as of this writing).

Or let's consider that other statement, "I'd like to take that person out on a date." From it came my desire to marry my wife

Danielle. Again, it began as an *idea* and then I became *lost*. That's the same process I have used for most of the successes in my life.

Was I the only one to ever have such a thought? No. Was *Outback* the first restaurant to ever have more than one location? Not by a long shot. After all, there aren't many "new" ideas, just different turns on others' concepts and wishes.

As there are pyramids around the world, it appears that building them wasn't a "new" idea for the Egyptians. *Disney-land* was spawned from an idea to create a clean, family- oriented amusement park but it wasn't the first type of "fair." *Coca-Cola* was just another soft –drink, and *Outback Restaurants* would be just another place to eat if not for one reason:

If those who had the ideas didn't get lost and leverage others, most, if not all, of those examples cited would not exist. That becomes the element that you need to understand.

Everybody has great ideas, but those ideas *need to be pursed until they come to be.* This fruition is the result of L.O.S.T.

To triple your results or success, remember the L.O.S.T. concept again, only this time the acronym becomes "leveraging others success triples."

What should you do if you get *lost* (most women know this answer)? You should ask for *directions.* Some may take longer than others to accomplish this feat, but by asking directions of themselves or of others, answers or strategies for getting what it is you want are provided.

Life gives you the opportunity to create whatever it is you want. *Accomplishment* is living out the ideas you have and having others help you get there. All you have to do is convince one person that your idea is great and live off your idea; then you will have success. When you get *lost* you have freedom. When you just have an *idea* and do nothing about it, chances are you will be left with frustration.

So then the question becomes, *do you want frustration or freedom?* Do you want to travel that last ten feet to the 10% Resort or are you happy being a 90 per center?

I can tell you now at this point in time you are a page closer to freedom and ten feet from your success, *so don't give up now.* I believe you want to be successful. So read on a little further. Your insight as to why you haven't become a success (yet) will be revealed, and then you will conquer what's holding you back. In the chapters that follow, success will be yours.

Chapter 5

1, 2, 3, Too Many: ~ How Your Brain Works

Picture this. It's 7:30 Thursday morning. A mother of three has the following to do.

A. Get dressed.

B. Get the children ready for school.

C. Make breakfast for her family

D. Put the kids in the car.

E. Drive them to school.

F. Stop by copy center and pick up her business presentation on the way to work

G. Be at the office by 9:30 a.m.

H. Put on an exciting presentation.

.

Sounds like an *exhausting* and not to mention a little *hectic* day is at hand. How do you think this woman's day would end up if she forgot something? The combinations could be endless. She could forget to put the kids in the car. She could miss going by the copy center. In any case, chances are it would no longer rank as one of her best days.

What about you? Have you ever had a day that created total chaos for you? Where one thing lead to another and then to another?

We all have had days that we wish we had stayed in bed. So why does these disastrous days happen? Are we humans' just prone to missing a step here and there? And is there anything that can be done about this? Yes, but let me clue you in on "why" we do the things we do.

Human beings are "wired" to be deletion creatures. We delete 97% of things going on in any given moment. You may not think about your heart beating or blinking your eyes, yet those things happen. They are automatic responses, and unless you start having a heart attack or something gets in your eye, chances are you won't give these processes a conscious thought. The same is true for the thousands of noises you can hear. If something grabs your attention, you will listen. Beyond that, your mind will view the sounds just as "noise." Mere sounds flowing together. Isn't your brain amazing?

This is all done as a means of survival. Wired into our subconscious, our focus to this day is the same as our ancestors. Food, clothing, and shelter, are not mere luxuries, but the essence of what it is we need to endure. That is why we don't have to will our hearts to beat or to think about seeing. Inside, these goals are handled for use so we can seek out the bare essentials of life, whatever they may be.

By allowing 3% of the material that surrounds us into our minds, we have accomplished several things. One is we can remember 1, 2, and 3. Most people can count to three. A good amount of us can summon up the first three digits of a phone number. But ask that same group for their drivers' license number ...and it's a complete blank. By design our brains see things as 1, 2, 3...*then too many*. Anything over "three" and our minds short-circuit in a sense.

This can explain the old acronym of K.I.S.S. and its misuse by millions of intelligent beings. In adding the fourth "s" (Keep it Simple, *Silly* or *Stupid*) our brains short out. We then forget to do what is asked of us, which is *keep things simple.*

Another benefit that this narrow band of focus provides is in the way we see things in our brain. In other words, our brain thinks in pictures. It's like me telling you to not think about a flying pig. In the processing of those words is the image of a flying pig. What is it wearing? Maybe a scarf or those funny goggles? I don't know, you tell me. After all, you are the one seeing it in your mind.

In spirit our brains are the great identifiers of our lives. From shapes to the hidden answer on *Wheel of Fortune,* we all have this built in computer that stores everything we experience. This stored experience creates reference points for us and helps us figure out how to approach certain issues and view certain things. Yet the data we put into this computer can be corrupt and distorted. When this happens, we tend to take on the "identity" of the situation. What does this mean?

Take what most of us avoid: failing. If you did something once and failed would it matter? Probably yes if it was something of great significance to you. Is that what people would think on the whole? Would you believe someone if they called you a failure then? Probably not. No, how <u>you identify yourself</u> is not by doing something only once or twice. The magic number usually turns out to be *three or more*. Now granted I am talking in a broad sense here, not a "once in a lifetime" event like an Olympian whose career can last a total of 30 seconds or less. Understand all Olympians are Successes, they are definably in the 10% club no matter where they finish, and anyhow I digress.

Being told something in repetition (three or more times) often helps create an internal identity exclusive to us. But the way this happens to each of us is unique. For some, it may take more than three times, while others may never believe what a situation renders. Each internal identity is just that: internal. You are never just one thing or another, but a mixture of elements all at once.

In fact, science has proven that beyond the initial acceptance of low repetition (3 or fewer times of seeing or being exposed to something which our brains take in), habits-things we tend to do repeatedly, are created by being exposed to things at least 21 times.

This is refreshing, in the sense that any bad habit you have can be replaced by doing something new 21 times. Want to try this?

For the next 21 days, place a note on top of your dresser or in your bathroom. On it write- place <u>(which ever is the opposite of your current leg) into my pants first</u>. If you put your right leg in then make the note say-put left leg in my pants first. Try it. After 21 days a new habit will be formed. What does this have to do with success? Everything!

You can retrain your brain to look for success. You can retrain or attract success into your life with repetition. *Steve G. Jones,* renowned in the field of Hypnotherapies suggest on all of his audio programs *"to listen for at least 21 days".* The same timeframe holds true for most other legitimate success coaches. Once isn't enough to gain what many have developed as habits over time. You need repetition to create new ways of thinking. This thinking becomes in a way your "new identity".

Yet there is a "fuel" that can speed up the process of identity. That fuel is called *emotion.* The more intense the emotion that is felt, the less time it takes a person to link to an event. A simple example of this is a song.

At my seminars I will often ask, *"How many can remember the song that was playing when they were making out for the first time?"* Quite a few of us can. Why?

In simple terms along with the intense emotions of the moment was the melody playing. The narrow band of conscious thought (3%) picked up on that song. The words, the chorus, the melody were just parts in a play entitled *"My Make out Song."* That song then becomes wired into our minds and in the future helps us to identify with that moment in time. When we hear the song on the radio, it will take us back to high school, lovers' lane, or some other passionate place. In that moment (or as in now) we can identify with whatever "title" we have associated with ourselves. That "title" or identity is as different as each moment we had. They all are unique and are "owned" by the individual.

For some- it was "prom" and the I was "a virgin".

Others- it was "a Friday night out" and I was "unfaithful".

Virgin, Unfaithful, even "Don Juan" are all terms created by the identity of a moment in time.

Interestingly, while the clarity of the picture created in our minds as a result of the association can be improved by the emotions we felt or feel, those same emotions also can *distort* the same picture as well.

In her book, *The 9 Steps for Financial Freedom,* author *Suze Orman* recalls the childhood of several clients. For some it was the events that transpired then influenced their future financial lives as adults. In one story, a woman remembers breaking a dinner platter. As the story goes, *"until she faced that memory, she hadn't realized her life was a reflection of that day."* This person would give large sums of money away, often sacrificing her own finances. Her actions were the result of trying to replace a broken plate, a Thanksgiving platter she had once shattered. She felt so bad for something that happened a long- time ago that, her life became a financial wreck.

From a personal case, there was a man who gave me great insight into this. I had helped him move towards becoming a *Ten* in his mind, *after helping uncover what was holding him back.*

The quitter-

Each day I would meet this man who would tell me, in great detail, how his life was a complete wreck. He told me of how miserable he felt, how he had let down his family .His marriage was over, he was fat, and he was broke. Then, as if that weren't depressing enough, he told me that throughout his entire life he had wanted to be more than what he was. He had, wanted to do great things, to be somebody. He wanted to be rich in friends and in finances; instead he was fat, poor and broke. He gave me the oddest look when I told him that "*being* that many things must have been exhausting." He didn't find my comment amusing, although I did.

This guy was an incredible emotional drain. But then, I finally asked him, sometime between his reasons and excuses for not feeling good or for not being a great person,

"What the hell is it that you want?"

His first answer was a resounding, *"I don't know."*

"Well, if you could do anything you wanted to do, what would it be?" I asked in an attempt to get this man to rise above his current state of depression.

He again responded, "I don't know", in a manner lacking any confidence.

This guy had started to annoy me. Here I was, dealing with his "pity party" when I could have been watching the Buc's play. However I managed to regain my composure and ask him to tell me about his childhood or anything that he could remember as standing out from those times. After all, I *was* there to help him.

The sense that he had experienced a wonderful childhood was evident. He told me of fishing trips with his father, his mom making biscuits and family outings to the lake each summer. There was no abuse, no horrific events that marred this man's early years. So I asked him to move beyond his childhood into his teens. He shared how he tried to "find himself" like every other teen in the world, which meant experimenting with cigarettes and alcohol. Again, no major red flags here; these are things "everybody does." So what else could be influencing this guy?

From his large physical size I knew he must have at least tried out for sports, so I asked him about that. Right then his eyes lit up, and he proceeded for the next hour of telling how great he was in wrestling and football. But within sports as within life, we all have coaches. I asked him to share his experiences from those who guided him. That's when the conversation changed.

"This coach in junior high was the biggest hard ass you'd ever seen," he said to me.

"How so," I asked.

Tears began to flow as he said, "This guy expected us to *know* how to play each position, but you first have to be taught the positions!"

"You didn't know how to play football?" I replied in a surprised tone.

"That's right," he answered back with his eyes red and full of hidden emotion.

"I knew you get the ball and run for touchdowns, but this guy didn't teach the team difference between a right guard and a tailback, so we were all lost."

On the first day of practice this coach cut five boys from the team. It wasn't for lack of talent, but for lack of knowledge. After they left, the coach told the team, "If you don't know how to play, you won't play for me."

Football for these guys was everything, so no one dared to speak up or complain. It was almost as if football was expected to be a part of these kids' DNA.

As the story continued I got a clear picture of this tyrant both on and off the field. Seemed when this coach wasn't busting *balls* on the field, he was ruining the lives of any boy who "liked" his daughter. Not to mention the fact that in those days "abuse" was a taboo word, so burning students with cigarettes was okay. As my mind created a picture of this demonic man, my client divulged an even darker image.

Because of the coach he decided to quit the team. This choice was hard for him to make. What would his parents think? His teammates? What would Coach do to him? Burn him, beat him or something worse?

"Some may think it would have been easier to stay on, but I couldn't," he told me. "I just couldn't take it anymore."

Like a man practicing the perfect presentation, he repeated to himself a thousand times beforehand, "Coach, I just can't do it anymore." And he decided to announce his departure on that Friday. This would give him two days of reprieve, and forty-eight hours to make up a convincing story of why he had to go.

On that Friday the bell rang and he walked the *green mile*. Walking past the showers into a smoke-filled office, he told Coach that he wouldn't be "available" for the team anymore. It was over. Well at least that part was.

The Coach grabbed him by the ear and dragged his flailing body out of the office. In any event, as the door shut behind them as hush of silence took over the otherwise rowdy team. All the boys stood there looking helpless. They were frozen in time at the sight of the crying boy attached to this coach's hand.

The coach made the boy repeat these four words to the team.

"I am a quitter."

"Again," this coach said, twisting the bloodied ear.

"I am a quitter," the boy complied, in a louder tone.

Then, as if to congratulate him, the coach released his ear. He then told the silent souls before them, *"Men, before you stand a quitter. This man will never complete anything in his entire life. He is abandoning you, me, and this team, for he feels he can't take it."*

With that, he dragged the boy outside of the locker room. The boy lay there, crying, as the salt from his tears stung the open wounds of his heart. The shame of quitting overshadowed his bravery to stand up for himself, and he never told a soul what he had done or experienced. Until this day.

That story became his dark secret… but it also became his redeemer.

You see, this story held the key to freeing this man from his "success amnesia." In finally recalling and recounting the painful memories this man discovered a certain truth, that his life, from that point in time of his past, to that moment in front of me, had been about one thing: *To prove that the coach had been wrong.*

But the story also unearthed something else, the reason why he quit the team in the first place. For him it had been a matter of not understanding something, and rather than ask questions (and risk the coach's ire) he decided he simply was not going to participate any longer. His life afterwards had become a reflection of those moments.

As an adult he would always choose to take on huge projects, but at the last minute they would fall apart, something he always inwardly expected. Why? He had been told he *"never would, that he was always going to quit."* Even though in the business world he was noted for being a risk taker, inside he was terrified and afraid to ask questions.

His life became a vicious cycle of never-ending risk- taking and never wanting to admit defeat. And until the day we talked and he recognized what had set the wheels in motion for him, things were not going to change. Inside he was always a *quitter*. A boy left alone on a grass field of despair.

We both cried when this was realized. But once we did, his life was forever changed. His life became an example of what is possible in each of us.

The End- or just a new beginning?

My purpose in sharing this story with you is this: If we know *why we are doing things then our lives begin to work.* Work in the sense of gaining some type of reward. We all do things that make complete sense to us most of the time, but at other times we do not.

When this happens we are left with a choice: We can do the things that make sense or we can try something else.

Success Side Note 11- *If we know the WHY- then our life begins to WORK better-* **if something doesn't work try something else- but you need to find the WHY.**

In my own life- I spent years building a business that made me miserable. My old logic was *"to prove that I could."* There were points in my life I avoided asking for help. Holding onto a faint memory of being ashamed, I kept silent. I married somebody whom I loved even though knew it wasn't going to work out, holding onto that relationship simply for *"not wanting to quit."* You see, that frail boy thrown out of a locker room was me. My life for a time was the result of fighting imaginary ideas, a set of events that some "coach" dumped into my head. But now one thing is different: Me.

I am no longer that frail boy. The days of those tears are behind me. When I realized that, things changed. I evicted the stupid identity of a scared child from my soul and moved my life into the place of success. That result <u>only</u> came from creating a life instead of living it.

You too can do the same. It comes from putting your heart and your mind together and resolving to be honest.

Success Side Note 12- *You can create your life instead of just living it*

Sincerity is crucial if you want to become successful. When your actions reflect your thoughts, success will arrive. Until that point, you will continue to chase a dream that may not come true.

I challenge you to take the same leap of faith I did. Stop chasing your dreams and discover what might be keeping you from them. If you'd like, I suggest doing the following exercise, you'll be amazed at the results.

Exercise – Liberate Your Success Amnesia

I suggest you first read through this and then complete the exercise. You can use these pages or get a notebook or something to capture your thoughts on. When completing, go find a quiet place away from the phones, the kids, the spouse, everybody. Once you are there, take three deep breaths.

With your lungs full of nice, clean air, I want you to think about your life. What do you have? A house, kids, cat? Or do you have nothing? Where are you are in your current pursuit of "success," and have you even figured out what it is you want? Write down your answers to these questions.

What do I have?
Where am I in my pursuit of success (close, far, haven't begun, still dreaming)?

Next, answer this. *What is one thing that has happened in my life that was horrible?*

I tell you, *it's easier to face it than it is to try to ignore (the horrible event that is).* So make it easy on yourself. Give the event a short, sweet title, like divorce, death, or bankruptcy. This way you won't have to stay there too long.

After that, I would like for you to capture the first three things you remember about the event. These can be anything: The date, the weather, or the people you were with. Capture those three things that stand out in your mind. Now look at these three things and notice how they affect your current life.

Below is an example of what your list may look like.

Step 1: **Things that I have:**

    Wife, kids, mortgage, credit cards…

Step 2: *One* **horrible thing that happened:**

    (Short but sweet title): *Divorce*

Step 3: *Three* **things about the event:**

    February, found a note, feeling of lonely

Sharing this exercise with several people, I have noticed a few things that are generally true. For instance, events that took place in a building leave an imprint on that person. One student feared hospitals.

Why? His mother died in one and he blamed it on the building. In other cases, as with dates, some feel bad the week prior to the event's anniversary. Others say that seeing certain people who were around at the time of the event always makes then feel horrible.

Here is the next part of the exercise: *What are some things that have occurred in your life since then (horrible event) that relate to the 3 things you have written about the event?* Capture those on paper. Here's an example or what it may look like you can use the next page to do this as well)-

Question 1- What I have? - *House, debt, maxed out credit cards.*

Question 2- Where am I towards success? - *Not even close*

Question 3- One horrible event in my life- *Cat was run over on my birthday*

Question 4- 3 things about that event-
a- miss my cat
b. cry on my birthday
c. eat lots of cake

Question 5- Things that have happened since that relate to the 3 things about the event-
1. I've gained weight
2. I've adopted 3 cats
3. My credit card debt has gone up

What I have?

Where am I towards Success?

One Horrible Event in my life-

3 Things about the event-

Thing that have happened that relate to the event-
(It's okay if you have a challenging time answering this question.)
The answer often lies in the next step of this process.

Since habits form from consistent action and thoughts, are there visible signs in your current life that you can now see spring from your past? There may be a few, although they may not jump off the page but take a moment and look at the example list and then apply the formula you learned from Chapter 2 (TBAR) –

Thoughts →Beliefs→Actions→Results. Do this by adding the letters to what you see as appropriate for each answer.

Example cont.-

What I have? - *House, debt, maxed out credit cards.* ← T/R

Where am I towards success? - *Not even close* ← B

One horrible event in my life- *Cat was run over on my birthday* - 3 things about that event-

a- miss my cat ← T   b. cry on my birthday ← A

c. eat lots of cake ← A

Things that have happened since that relate to the 3 things about the event-

4. I've gained weight ← R
5. I've adopted 3 cats
6. My credit card debt has gone up

Since our Thoughts Lead to our Beliefs then our Action and our Results, which circle back to our Thoughts, we must draw a line connecting them.

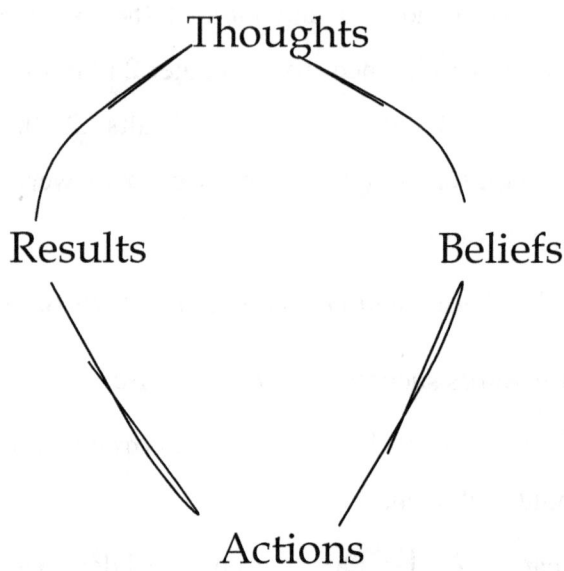

Once the lines are matched, you can begin to see what may have been occurring in your own life. Some experiences I have been fortunate enough to witness from this have been seeing those whom have *piled huge amounts of debt (a Result- R),* and in doing this exercise, realize that the burden of debt gave them a *sense of responsibility (Thought-T).* They felt they *needed to spend (Action-A)* as a way to show that they could pay off the debt and in doing so, could *win the respect of their spouse (Belief –B)* or someone else. In another case, with a troubled teenager, the exercise proved to that their "bad behavior" was extended from a feeling of boredom. What about you?

Can you see or begin to link where your success has been hiding by the formula and exercise? You may have to do this a few more times with a few more memories until you start to see what habit's you've formed in your life.

It is important to understand the simple reasoning and define what each part of the formula represents.

THOUGHTS- Anything that you think of.

BELIEFS -Any thought you have WITH conviction of extended feeling.

ACTION- Any step YOU may take or NOT Take that reinforces your belief

RESULT- Residual effects of Action, Beliefs, and Thoughts reflected in your mind. These can also become Thoughts (such as debt etc).

Once you do, there is a step you can take to begin reversing any "bad" behavior you may notice from this exercise. It's what I call *"The Relinquisher."*

Exercise- Be "The Relinquisher"

To accomplish '*The Relinquisher*," take the sheet of paper on which you've written down your horrible incidents, and it's related memories, outside. (If you have done this on these pages, please don't take the book outside, copy your answers onto a piece of paper).

Find a place that is open and airy. Now, read what you've written to yourself one more time. After you've read it, close your eyes. Think back to that time. Once you are there, tell your memory, "thank you." Thank the event for shaping your life. Thank it and be grateful for it. Once you have come to peace with the memory, take the paper and burn it (carefully, of course; be sure not to start a fire!). Watch the ashes flicker into the air along with the days that are now behind you. When you do this, *"The Relinquisher"* will be *you*. You will be moving ahead *without* the past holding you back.

Whatever the event was in your life, I can tell you that you're now okay. You made it this far. Life now equals success for you. There are no longer any reasons to feel bad, although I understand if you do. Just remember as time passes we can learn to put things away. We can hide them in our routines as if they had never happened.

For some this exercise of relinquishment can prove painful. In one instance a gentleman got up and stormed out of the room, telling me *"I had no business to stir up those memories."* It was that point that I realized how much we avoid something that serves us, which is pain. The eventual thing we try to escape in our lives gives us the power to grow.

Pain is that ache in our chest telling us we need to go to the doctor. Pain is that low number in our checking account urging us to create more wealth, not spend it on an indulgence. Pain is that someone walking out the door, when saying, "I love you" to them a few more times may have kept them there. Pain serves us when we heed its message.

It also serves us in other ways. You see pain puts us in a place of "success expectation." "Success expectation" is *the result of those things at which you have spent a good amount of time doing.* This in and of it self is neither all good nor all bad, but a way that helps create our behaviors. In others words, you've gotten good at avoiding your "painful" memory. As a result of this avoidance, you've come to expect a certain kind of success. That student of mine who feared hospitals? He gave me this explanation for his "success expectation": *"Well if I don't go to the hospital, I won't die. You see my mother died at a hospital, so I won't go."* He expects success…as a result of his pain, and in a roundabout he way gets it.

From my own personal example, I expected to finish something (well, anything) so I could prove my coach "wrong." That inner drive was part of what brought about these words you are reading now. It was that same desire to "prove" I could which led me to continue on with some projects (some of which I should have quit!)

All of the above examples are success expectations. It's a nice way to let you in on what you've been doing, and a way to discover some of the benefits. Benefits as with my student, can tell you where every hospital is in a twenty mile radius. As with me, I have the tenacity of a bulldog. You see, I believe all behavior, good or bad, is in the end, good. That's because it serves us. However, being *"The Relinquisher"* of your old thoughts is critical to get past what has held you back. By doing so, you become acquainted with another power: The part of you that has "protected" you. How?

By seeing once and for all what drives you. Your inner drive is the part of your being that creates the importance of things in your life.

Success Side Note 13- *Change your Success Expectations, Change your Life!*

If you'd like to explore what exactly your Success Expectations have been- answer the following-

- What else has this avoidance provided me with?
- Can you see some benefits from the "pain" of your past?
- Are you a better person because of it? For example, do you choose not to quit because of what has happened in your past?

The benefits and the insight you gain will help you move forward to your success, so make sure to write them down. *When you begin to align what you hoped to get from the past with what you want now from the future, your success then begins to take shape.*

Success Side Note 14 - *Those who are successful has aligned their beliefs with the results that they want.*

As a Ten, you may see that things that were important once are no longer now, and those small things that you once gave no thought to have had the greatest impact on your life. *Success first comes from a thought, then from a conscious understanding of what goes on in and around us.* This often is the opposite of what many try to sell us. What we are sold is the Process for Success Reversal (from Chapter 2) - or TARB (Thought-Actions-Results-Beliefs).

From *lose-weight-today diets* to *making millions in real estate courses*, every day we are bombarded with hundreds of ways to ease the "pain." There's a discomfort that lies inside each of us, and many of us think the answer to their problem comes *from* someone else, when, in fact it, comes from *inside. There are no external answers or causes- they are all within YOU!*

With that said the answers to your success don't live within these pages; they lie within *your answers to the exercises.*

Finding painful memories is not what other gurus want you to do (at least from my experience). And most don't even take the time to help you realize the way things work. But being resourceful isn't so much about knowing a lot of things as it about *understanding what works.* Many will say they aren't successful and/or don't see it for themselves. That's because they don't realize what works.

Success Side Note 15 - *Knowing what works gives you clarity- clarity is not an external occurrence.*

A simple fact to remember is that we tend to say "no" to what we don't understand. "No" is the defense mechanism our brain uses to protect us from things. "No" is more than a word; it is, a feeling inside. The feeling of "no" is felt when we are not accepting a subject or a change.

"NO"

NOT UNDERSTAND = NO ENJOYMENT = WON'T DO IT.

If a telemarketer calls you during dinner, what's the first thing you say? *No.* That's because you may think that this person is "violating" your time or space. They could be giving you a million dollars, but that doesn't matter to you. On some level you are saying to your-self, "I don't understand how they can call now and interrupt my dinner." So, in the end you won't buy from, or even listen to, the person at the other end of the phone. "No" becomes the silent partner in the back of your mind that tells you to hang up on that person even if they offering you something of value (which many times they are not). It is such a powerful word and feeling that many times we don't realize how close success is to us …and that we have shut it out by saying "No".

Understanding How Change Works

Think of the many books, programs, or courses you have taken or purchased over the past few years. Or even the schoolbooks you read from days and years ago. Have you applied *everything* you have learned from them? If you had assimilated all of the knowledge, techniques, and information presented in those materials, can you say that things might be different in your life? *I would bet my life that each of our lives would be very different right now if we had understood and appreciated everything life has taught us up to this point.* There are a ton of great books, programs and even "products" that can and do make our life easier (including this one). Our life can be so "easy" at times; we take for granted everything we have at our disposal. Many times we will say "no" to the things that will provide us with the success we desire and yes to frustration and despair. Why? The answer is a simple phrase told to me by *Jim Rohn,* America's pre-imminent motivator, which says, "people know what to do, but rarely do what they know."

Maybe if we had *thought* about some of the things we have done before we did them and said, "yes" instead of "no" to a few others, our lives would be different. However, we can't live in yesterday (although many still do). We can't go back to the 6th grade or retry that missed field goal. However, while we can't change the past we *can* prepare for the future.

Preparing begins from right now, and moves you forward. It's a journey of understanding that you have already begun by picking up this book. And you have started to walk the walk by doing the exercises. For its *understanding* that's the key to it all.

More often than not we get so caught up in the day-to-day things that we fail to see what we want. Many find solace in a drink or a cigarette. Some eat or shop their troubles away. They miss the point of it all. They wake up one day wanting a change… but not knowing how.

Change, large or small, comes from understanding. Understanding comes from a desire to learn. Desire, for many, is the wanting of more in their life and yet it is this same thing we call *desire* that in many cases creates what we call "failure." Many will say that we fail when we don't get what we desire. Yet desire isn't the *root* of failure, but a *measuring device* for it.
Failure itself comes from three areas in ones life. I call these areas "reasons." They are as follows.

Failure Happens Because Of:
- Reason #1   too many steps
- Reason #2   not understanding the steps
- Reason #3   not deciding in the first place

What success is? To them

Forget the childhood excuses about a dysfunctional family being at the root of failure! Erase thoughts of *"I'm not good enough or smart enough"* as it relates to doing whatever it is you want to do. If you want to know a good reason why you are reading this and not living what you want your successful-life to be, it is because of these three reasons. Somewhere you made things (notice I said _you_, not your boss, ex-husband, kids, parents, _but you_) more challenging than they needed to be.

I know that's a pretty harsh reality to accept. You may have read other books out there that tell you a host of other reasons behind why and how to get success, but it boils down to you and those three areas of failure. Don't be defensive and say, *"Yes, but my life is not so bad; it's not like I'm living in the streets in a cardboard box."* Well, that may be the case, but are you living the life you want to be? *Take a moment and move beyond what your life is now, and think about what you want your life to be.*

Being resourceful isn't so much about knowing a lot of things but understanding what works. We go to school to learn, to understand. We buy books. Attend seminars and research on the internet. Millions of eyes are searching for this one item of information. But we're living in a fantasyland.

Success Side Note 16- *Being Resourceful is being Successful*

The big lie that many of us were taught says, *"Information is power."* Information is just that: Information. Its *potential* power but not power itself. You have the power and the ability to create the success you want. You can exercise this power by saying, "Yes, I can" or "No, I won't." If you've done any of the exercises so far, then in essence you are saying yes. If you have read the exercises and glanced over them with the thought of "I'll do it later", then inside you are saying no. I won't judge you for taking either road, but I would like to expose you to another truth that may enlighten you on how success can be created. Saying "no" becomes the backdrop for failure, but so is lack of understanding.

As with the first reason of failure: *too many steps.* Making things larger than they have to be is a common act among those who fail. They tend to look at all of the steps combined into this massive undertaking and never move a muscle. Success becomes "too much" of an undertaking to pursue.

The second step of failure, or *not understanding the steps,* is another culprit. Many people don't do things or attempt to do things for they don't understand them. Until I wrote this book, I was intimidated by the mere magnitude of what goes into publishing. I didn't understand the steps it took to write a good book, get an agent, or even find an editor. Consequently, this book for the longest time was just a distant dream written amongst notes of a journal.

Then there is one of the more subtle reasons for failure: *Not deciding what success is in the first place.* Because it is subdued in every day actions, most won't recognize it or worse yet, call it something else. Many go through life labeling this affliction with failure as being *unlucky.* However, it's the farthest thing from the truth.

By not deciding in the first place what you want your outcome to be, you are at the mercy of the events that surround you. For instance, if you were invited to go to a party, would you decide what to wear after you got there? I'd venture to say, no. Depending on the event, you determine what kind of outfit you will wear before you leave the house. You wouldn't want the embarrassment of showing up in a costume if it was a formal dinner? But what about the real reason for attending this party, have you given thought to that?

The real reason, or what you hope to gain, is why you are going. Most of us do things to feel better, or "to have a good time." Yet, if you didn't consciously decide to enjoy yourself at this party, you could walk away miserable. You could arrive and then spend the evening focused on a couple that is arguing or find yourself alone with no one to talk with. By not determining what you want your success to be (in anything large or small), failure has a greater chance of happening.

That is why I keep repeating the fact; *first decide what it is you want and then become clear about it.* The rest of this book will only help you if you have a clear goal in mind. That is why you need to do the exercises. I can't stress that point enough. If you believe you are ready to move forward because you have a clear goal in mind, first let me share one more personal insight into the way we think. It comes in the form of another quick exercise.

Success Side Note 17- *Make the Impossible Possible*

Exercise- Word Transformation

All that is needed for this exercise is for you to read and absorb the following words.

Would you like a million dollars? If your answer is yes, then I want to give you the opportunity to make a million dollars by answering 3 simple questions. *If you answer the three questions, the money is yours, no strings attached. Sound good?*

What if I told you that the questions are about something very familiar to you (i.e. say your name, spell it, and tell me your initials)? My guess would be that you would have no problem answering them, or taking the million dollars? *Is that right?*

How about if I told you that in order to get the million dollars **you would have to answer the questions in <u>fewer</u> than 30 seconds, and the questions would be about something so <u>unfamiliar to you</u>, that even guessing would be <u>useless?</u> Winning that million dollars would become "<u>impossible</u>" in your mind. <u>Receiving that check becomes impossible in your reality.</u>**

The exercise is over but the explanation begins.

First, since this is a reading exercise and not a live event, I can point out the obvious conditioners for the exercise. I purposely underlined the "negative" text, giving your focus to the "impossible" and otherwise disempowering words.

This is why so many people stay in the 90% club and never achieve the success they deserve or even want. They think "impossible," and their life becomes a reflection of that thought. They allow the three reasons for failure to control their lives. Every day they are quizzed by life on what they in fact want, and they fail to get it by 1. *Creating too many steps,* 2. *Not understanding the steps* and 3. *Not deciding what they want in the first place.* If you would like to remove the influence of these steps from your life, then do this short little exercise.

First, say the word "impossible" out loud. Brings you down, doesn't it? Now take the same word and separate it into three sounds. "I-M-Possible" or "I'm possible." Say that out loud. Does it feel different? Almost *promising?*

I'd be willing to bet the next time you thought something was "impossible" and you stepped back and looked at it instead as "I'm possible," there would be a different outcome. Somewhere inside "I'm possible" is the greater you. The "you" that can accomplish much more than you think. The "you" that has done things in the past that were great.

Everybody has done at least one great thing in his or her life, whether it's something as simple as offering a smile to a stranger or opening a door for someone. It could have been helping a turtle cross a busy highway or taking a stray animal in. Whatever it may have been, inside of you at that moment, you told yourself "I'm possible" and *you were.* You made that one great thing happen... so why not tap back into that power again? All it is saying to yourself what you know to be true; *that you are an example of what is possible.*

This isn't about positive thinking or motivation. This is about *going with your instinct that tells you for once in your life you can begin to change,* even if it is by looking at a word or situation in a different light and feeling a little spark inside.

That's what the Tens of the world do. They look at things, and understand those things in a different version than the rest of us do.

How? Well, for the lack of a technical term, it's called "chunking," which is nothing more than grouping or separating something into far more manageable parts. From these groups or parts, the Tens see things with distinction and decide what area they can handle and what areas they need to have a partner to help them with. (We will be covering partnerships later). Ninety per centers do the opposite.

They take something (like making a million dollars) and think of all the things that need to be done in order to obtain "the goal." They don't even realize that for every part of the process there is somebody that can do it for them. The creed for many ninety per centers is, *"If you want something done right, you have to do it yourself."* The creed of many Tens is, *"If you want something done right, hire that person to do it for you."*

Success Side Note 18- *If you want something done right- hire that person to do it for you*

The Tens of the world aren't so different from us; they just think another way, which leads to a refreshing fact that we all must remember.

Those who are successful have the same kind of brain that unsuccessful people have.

I know brilliant people who are dumb as hell and morons who are borderline geniuses in what they have accomplished. So, how does a successful person think? Well one answer lies in the 10% Solution. Come along with me into the next chapter and I will show you how this 10% solution can change the way you think, and how it can help you get whatever it is you want out of life.

Success Side Note 19- *We are all cut from the same successful cloth of those before and after us- I am a SUCCESS, I'M Possible.*

Kayton Kimberly

Chapter 6
The *10% Solution:* The Aladdin's Lamp to Your Problems

There are countless versions of the *magic genie* story. All in all there's the genie, an apparition that is sealed away for doing something wrong, cursed to an eternity of living behind glass.

Then there's the unsuspecting person who finds the bottle in which the genie is contained. Usually it's an average "mortal" who is now faced with 3 chances to get the life they want. Will they choose riches? Love? Fame? It really doesn't matter what they wish for, as most times the "wishes" are misused, and all that's left are the thoughts of what could have been.

But that isn't real life. *Cinderella* and *Pinocchio* aren't any more real than a genie in a bottle. And as much as we want to believe, we know that fairy tales aren't true. The characters in them receive the perfect ending. Their lives created simply for us to dream about and learn from.

From *Aladdin's Lamp* to *Rocky* and *Star Wars*, each story that moves us is about victory. Every great tale throughout time has this element of man overcoming "something." It can be himself, his surroundings, or an evil power that wants to control him. It is this same power he draws upon that can become the source of your success. Inside of you resides the power to conquer any challenge you may face.

This overcoming of obstacles can be called many different things: Willpower, perseverance, or as in the movie *Jerry Maguire, "the Quan."* That dynamic is that each of us has the power to overcome and surpass any obstacle, if we in fact *really want to.*

The *"really want to"* part seems to be where a lot of people get into trouble. It's easy to say, "Show me the money." but for most, it's hard to do or achieve. A good number get caught up in advertently creating too many obstacles that interfere with their success. As we discussed in the last chapter, "too many" has a way of deterring our success instead of creating it. However there is a way to overcome this… and it is called *the 10% Solution.*

It is named after a concept taught to me from author *Dr. Robert Schuller*, which states *that there are no less than 10 solutions to a problem.* Dr. Schuller utilized this concept to create the Crystal Cathedral, a massive "glass" church in California. He also used this process several times in creating answers to problems where as many would have thought to say were "impossible."

In his book, *Tough Times Don't last, but Tough People do*, he tells of how, when beginning his service to God, he was without money, a church or even a congregation. He did, however, have a family to support. Troubled, he found himself sitting in a diner. At a point half way between security and destiny, he contemplated his dilemma. Though it may have been easier to "give up," that wasn't his purpose.

Dr. Schuller knew his calling was to preach. That was his *idea*. Within the "silenced thoughts" he solidified the idea of his life's purpose. He was to share the word of God with the world no matter what. It didn't matter if he had no church or a congregation. He was on a mission. He was getting *lost*.

What happened? As he said, *"something told him to grab a napkin and write the numbers one to ten."* Once he did, he began to think of ten places he could hold gatherings. Ideas of buildings, clubs, movie theatres and even a funeral home flowed from his mind. These were places that he could preach from. His focus wasn't on money or a congregation just a place to do what he was destined to do. That was the genesis for the *"10 % Solution"* as he named it.

Within my own life I myself have utilized this same process hundreds of times. For example, this book, at some level is a result of the 10% Solution because one day I sat down and wrote out ten different ways to market it. At other times in my life, when I was feeling "down," I would write ten things I was happy about and by the time I got to number ten, I realized I was feeling pretty good. When I was dead broke and couldn't make my car payments or even afford to put food in my belly, I sat down and figured ten ways I could earn extra cash. When I went through my divorce, I utilized the 10% Solution to help me focus on what I wanted my next relationship to be about. There isn't a part of my life that hasn't been affected in a positive manner by this solution, and after researching the lives of other successful people; I learned that they too have applied the same technique to their lives as well.

Andrew Carnegie, the founder of U.S. Steel, called his principle a "mastermind alliance." Inventor Henry Ford called his *"these buttons on my desk."* Jesus called his "disciples." These successful people would find their solutions to problems within the knowledge and spirit of others as well as themselves. Their answers came in the form of real results that were seen and recorded. Examples of this are Carnegie creating top quality steel at prices unheard of in his market, and Ford creating transportation for the "masses."

Success Side Note 20- *You find solutions in the Spirit of Others as well as yourself.*

The fact is, like Dr. Schuller, I myself didn't have the resources of several people at the beginning of my success journey either. What the 10% Solution gave me was the power *to look inside and find the answers that I needed*. This brings up another point.

No matter where you start from, it always begins with you. The great successes of the world are no different than you. Remember that each of us are already a success, life has given that to each of us. The answers to what eludes us aren't in books or in seminars, but inside ourselves. We find the answers that are presented to us (from books, tapes, speeches or what many call outside sources) but in the end, they all come from inside.

For example, actor *Sylvester Stallone* was turned down over 200 times by acting agents in New York. Restaurant entrepreneur *Colonel Sanders* was told over 1,000 times, *"No thanks; we already know how to fry a chicken."*

From encountering each of these rejections, both men knew that they needed one "yes" to set in motion events that would provide them with that "extra 10%" of what they desired.

For Stallone, his encounters with rejection proved the genesis for reaffirming the fact he wanted to be an actor. For the Colonel, it provided him a way to increase his earnings beyond his meager social security check. Similarly, for everyone who has ever moved from the 90 percent club into the 10% Resort, the 10% Solution was at work in some way (though most would not call it that). *Each step we take towards success is an answer to a question that is asked of ourselves.* The 10% solution places the questions and answers at a conscious level so that things are easier to see, understand and apply.

That is the real benefit of the solution itself. *By placing things out in the open and getting you to think about answers to problems, you then begin to tap into your own will- power.* When that happens, your life begins to change at a rapid pace.

Do you think you can handle this kind of change in your life? Do you want to begin to utilize the same tools the Tens of the world do? Who knows, with a little practice you may even become a Ten!

With this in mind, let us take the concept on a trial run so you can get the concept down and begin to think like a Ten. If you are ready, I would like to show you *How to Make a Million Dollars.*

How to Make A Million Dollars

1) Earn $500,000 a year for 2 years

2) Cure Cancer

3) Sell 20 $50,000 products

4) Sell 4 $250,000 products

5) Win a lottery jackpot worth $1,000,000

6) Marry Britney Spears

7) Play golf like Tiger Woods

8) Finally figure out why men/women do the things they do

9) Make $40,000 for 25 years

10) Become an *American Idol*

What you have read is an example of the 10% Solution. Simple and easy, isn't it? Well, yes and no. To the naked eye, it would seem viable that any of those solutions could indeed create a million dollars, but there is a catch. If you look back at the list, notice how many things are related. Other than selling a certain amount of products, none of these solutions have any relevance to each other, other than then end result of making a million dollars

For example, look at # 6, marry Britney Spears. Other than the result (i.e. making a million dollars), how is that related to say #10, or becoming an *American Idol?* The relevance is nil. Sure, one has a better shot of marrying Ms. Spears if they are of celebrity (or of a dance crew i.e. Kevin Federline), but the answers themselves need to solutions that *you can create.* The optimal 10% solution is one that has *a balance between the outrageous and the practical.*

Somewhere between those two points, the process itself becomes an exercise in brainstorming and *utilizing personal experience.* In general, when I am utilizing this process I will allow the first 2 to 5 answers to be for "big" answers, and then I will make the remaining answers smaller, more do-able versions of the larger ones. Let me show you in this example. On the following page I'm going to give a real life version of how to create a millions dollars! No magic wand, no infomercials here, but 10 real ways to make One Million dollars.

How I can create a Million Dollars

1.) Does one thing for 1 million dollars
2.) Does two things at $500,000 each
3.) Does four things at $250,000 each
4.) Does five things at $200,000 each
5.) Does 10 things at $100,000 each
6.) Does 20 things at $50,000 each
7.) Does 100 things at $10,000 each
8.) Does 2000 things at $500 each
9.) Does 5000 things at $200 each
10.) Does 200,000 things at $5.00 each.

There you go: one of those ways now is how I can create a million dollars, and how *you can as well*. Let me ask you, *how many other books have you read that tell you how to make a million bucks and give you real solutions to do it*? Not many, I'm sure, but perhaps you are sitting there thinking, "Sure, this list looks great but I have no clue what to do 5000 times to make $200 each time." Well, I didn't either when I wrote this list, but then I did what is the real secret is to this solution.

The Secret to the 10% Solution

The secret to the 10% Solution that is somewhere between the numbers one and ten I repeated the step (10% solution-10 ways to get a result) and determined *what I could do for each of those solutions to create that type of financial windfall.*

For example, as I wrote this list, I realized that I wasn't an actor. Nor had I invented any *one* thing that could make a million dollars (answer # 1). The same held true for # 2-6. But then as I moved on in the list, I began to recognize a few facts. I remember a few times in my life I had made $10,000 (#7) for repossessing incredibly valuable equipment (such as a yacht and an airplane). From that experience, I began to think how I could locate and repossess 100 of these things. When I considered #8, I realized I had done several things in my life that had earned me $500.00, and again, I thought about ten different ways to expand upon that process. The most challenging answers came with coming up with what could fulfill the #10 "solution" or making $5.00 200,000 times.

I asked myself about the first time I made $5.00? After a short ride down memory lane, the answer came to me: Mowing the neighbor's grass. But $5.00 here and $5.00 here only gets you so far. If I mowed five yards a day, I would make $25.00 daily- but $25.00 a day it would take me 109 *years* to earn a million dollars. This made me realize that if I were to make a million "five at a time" I was going to have to creative and that it would help to see what others have done to get the same result.

Getting 200,000 people to part with $5.00 may seem a daunting task, but it's everyday occurrence. Think of how many people eat at a fast-food restaurant or buy a book on a given day. If you filled your car up with gas in the past week, I'm sure it costs you more than $5.00. How many other people did the same?

The real key to this is to remember *that for everything you wish to accomplish, there is someone, somewhere that can help you do it.* There is another point as well and that is *whenever you spend, some one else earns.* That rule is what makes the world of finance possible.

It's also what works in the spiritual world as well, for spending your time with those who love you creates bonds far more important that any financial gains could be.

Success Side Note 21- *Keeping Others in Mind is the fastest way to expand your success*

Thinking about making a million dollars will only get you so far. Thinking how a Millions will help you, your family, friends and loved ones will get you a little further. Thinking how the world will be better because of your "value" (in both monetary *and spiritual meanings)* can determine not only what goal you want to accomplish but the beliefs behind it. Remember- *Successful people have their beliefs aligned with their actions and results.* Think about things not only from not your personal earning experience, but from the perspective of what you are willing to give to others as well.

Now that you have been exposed to the 10% solution and a few ways I have utilized it, let's try it together and see what results you can come up with.

Exercise- A Practice Run at the 10

Your exercise is as follows:

Find a notebook, a journal, or a piece of paper. At the top, write a word or sentence expressing a problem you would like to solve.

Next, write the numbers 1 to 10 down the left side of the page.

Now after each of those numbers, write something that *can* be done (not what you can or can't do at this time) to get that result. Repeat the process until you have all ten spots filled in. Remember; utilize your imagination and experience: if it can be dreamt of, then it can be done.

Go back now and look at your list. Does a certain item or two stands out as a possible solution? Is there one answer, one solution that looks like it may be worth spending your time and effort completing? If you find such an answer but still don't know where to go with it, take the answer and place it the top of the page. Then write down ten solutions or things can be done to achieve that goal. By repeating the process until one finds a realistic and do-able option, you can find limitless ways to solve problems.

This limitless supply of solutions can be expanded beyond your own personal world into other areas as well. As a parent, you can use the process to teach your children a simple technique that will serve them throughout their lifetime. Companies can teach their employees effective ways to create solutions to problems that they may be experiencing. The applications are as diverse as the issues that can be solved with this. So, if you do no other exercise in this book but this one, I can almost guarantee you will never look at your problems the same way again. And that new perspective will put you on the path to being a Ten. *That path is created by the answers that lie between the numbers one and ten.* Within those steps is the freedom to create your success.

Imagine for a moment if you applied this 10% solution to every "problem" in your life... how long would it take to solve major issues? Not long at all. With practice, you can even help solve the problems of others as well! So, go ahead, use the 10% Solution. Find no less than ten ways to create the success your life deserves. Inside each solution is a virtual roadmap that you can create that will lead to your success. By doing this again and again you will stop focusing on what isn't working and begin to do the things that will yield positive results. Also within the context of doing the 10% Solution you may also discover the reason you do the things you do.

Chapter 7

The Power of Why

Have you ever experienced a child asking the question *"Why?"* over and over again? *"Why* is the sky blue? *Why* can't I have ice cream? But- *why, why, why?"* The first few times it's almost amusing watching them act in a curious state of discovery. After twenty times, it becomes irritating. I myself have a low threshold for children asking *"why?"* My limit is about four times, and then it's back to the parents with them.

Often times I have seen when adults are confronted with this situation, they will fall back to the "authority" standpoint and answer, *"I'm the mommy (or daddy) and that is why."* They've crumbled under the constant pressure to provide complex answers to simple questions. Have you ever seen or experienced such a situation? When things like this happen, an interesting fact comes to light.

When a question of "why" is asked, our brains search for an answer even if it doesn't have one. Each person has a different tolerance for the speed at which the answer is provided. This variance can create a sense of comfort or a sense of urgency. In other words, if I asked you to answer several questions and gave you plenty of time to respond, you would feel comfortable. On the other hand, if I asked you to answer questions in what surmounted to a "lightning round" of *Jeopardy*, your body would react, creating a level of "stress" that wouldn't be comfortable. It's this uncomfortable feeling that helps create the "impossible" feeling inside, and it's that feeling which helps "protect" you from the pain you feel may be coming.

Amazing how all of this, and more, comes from the power of why. Those three little letters are the essence of what our lives become. *"Why"* is the reaction and cause for many of the thoughts we have, in fact, we can connect every chapter in this book to the power of why. From placing a number 10, to imagining flying pigs, to saying I'm possible, and even to you reading this far is the result of "why." You wanted to have success and somewhere inside you asked yourself, "Why?" The answer you received placed this book in your hands. Beyond that (and the reason for this chapter) is to let you know that "why" can be a great tool to utilize in your successful life.

Motivate Your Life with "Why"

Without spending an entire book on the subject of how and why the human brain works (there are plenty of those on the market already), I would like to offer you one pure formula to remember when it comes to the dynamics of your thoughts. Once you commit this to memory and utilize some of the other tools you have been exposed to, I can say with almost certainty your life will explode into a realm of possibility you never knew existed.

Are you ready for the ultimate secret of why? Can you handle what most every thought you have ever had is about? If the answer is yes, then read the following and commit it to memory.

W.H.Y. = Will Help You

That is what your brain is designed to do, help you get whatever it is that you want. *When you ask "why" of things you get the answers you are searching for.* <u>That is the power of you.</u> You and you alone control the thoughts and the reactions you will have to the answers that result from "why" questions. If you get upset (like a parent who snaps at a child for asking "why?" too many times), then you have given up all power to that person.

Success Side Note 22- *The more power you give to others the less you will have for yourself. This in turn will give you less of the things you need.*

Often, I hear people say, *"Gosh, I don't have the willpower to do something (quit smoking, save money, lose weight)."* When I hear this, I ask them why. You know what happens next? A bunch of excuses, with an "outside" source related to it.

For example, they will tell me things like, *"I can't quit for my friends still smoke."* Or, *"I can't lose weight for my husband likes to eat out all of the time."* In those two sentences, one can almost see that the power of the individual has been given up to someone else. To correct this, all one needs to do is notice that willpower begins with *will*. Don't think of it as "will" as in "willpower" but as "the will of the individual." After all that is the first element of W.H.Y. <u>**Will.**</u>

The sooner decisions are made and acted upon by the same person (in other words, once someone begins to use their will power), the faster the power of why will grow. That is why it is called "willpower" and it leads to the second letter or the *help* part of why.

<u>**Help**</u> is nothing more than someone admitting that they can't do something by themselves and can use support from someone or something else.

Remember back in *Chapter 4* when we discussed getting L.O.S.T.? What was the first thing we should do to get lost? Ask for directions. That is getting help. We know that we will need assistance, so we ask for it. Remember, this is the real way in nature has designed us to work. We have untapped abilities that improve our lives and others through the things we accomplish.

Success is life and this is another example. Tapping into the power of "why" can change your life but only if you decide on something that you want to change. Inside that change is your success waiting to be released. That success can be utilized by the assistance of others.

In the end, that is the third letter and purpose of WH**Y**: to help **you.** If you haven't done it yet, this is the place to decide what you want your success to be. But do yourself a favor: ask and answer only one thing for the moment. Don't attempt to figure out what you want your entire life to be about. Focus on *one* success right now. It will make things easier to understand, and the goal to *accomplish.* That is why so many programs don't work; they ask you to figure your entire life in 30 minutes or 30 days.

Success Side Note 23- *You are free to desire many things, but focus upon one success at a time*

The fact is, we all evolve as our wants, needs and desires do. Things change. What we want today is accomplished tomorrow, and then what? Many decide on something new to dream of or go after. That is life. So, make this point in time easy on yourself and decide on only *one* thing you would like.

Maybe it's a dream, (like a career), a thing (like a car), or a feeling (like to be in love with someone). What ever it is, write it down now.

With that "it" in mind, instead of figuring out how to get what you want right now, (which becomes easy with the 10% Solution), let's find out the *why* for it.

The reason this step is so important is that by determining "why" we want something, we can determine what we hope to get from it. From this we can decide if we do, in fact, want it. So many times, we decide we want something, make a plan for getting that goal and obtain the goal. Then the question or feeling: *Is this it? Is this all there is?* emerges.

Have you ever experienced that? The feeling of getting what you wanted and then having it fade away? It's like buying a new car or a new dress and being excited about the item… but then the "newness" wears off. I believe this is something we all have experienced, and yet think of the things in your life right now that you wouldn't give up for *anything*. These things more often than not were the result of thinking about a goal and appreciating them when they were obtained. Things like your grandparent's china set or your children can't be replaced that harbors the real answers of "Why?" You see if I were to ask you, "Why won't you sell me your china set for $200 or give up your children?" I am sure you would offer some convincing reasons for not giving any of these "priceless" items up (well, except for the kids!). Most would say "not for money, not for anything." That happens because everything in our lives right now and in the future that we find priceless is the result of us being attached to them with strong emotions.

Even when your kids are driving you crazy or you want to throw grandma's platter at your husband you refrain because you, at some level, really like the things you have. But what happens if you aren't thrilled with something? Can the opposite happen? Yes.

The Emotion Behind it All

The truth is, if we aren't getting what "we want" from something; we will drop it at a moment's notice. Think of a job that you may have quit or a relationship that went bad. No matter what exactly happened, you were removed from the situation (either through your own will or by the will of another) because there was an emotional need that was not being met. This is the reason why we date each other or go to a bunch of job interviews. No matter the situation we all are looking to fill an emotional need.

Those who are always looking for the "right" job believe that a new job or situation is the key to happiness, so they quit and start over again. They say things like "I love this new job" and then quit a month later because the boss was a "jerk." Upon examination, the boss at the four other jobs this person quit were "jerks" as well. The solution for finding a job at which one will stay put as well as for finding lasting success comes from "why."

By asking "why" or what do we hope to get from this (the job, relationship, new car purchase, etc.) we establish or create an emotional connection, which forms results. Don't believe me, then why is there always a group of those who are unemployed? Their needs (emotional) are not being met.

There isn't a job unfilled in this world that someone, somewhere can't do; the problem is that many feel that certain jobs aren't for them. The position is unfilled is that each person feels that the job won't provide what he or she wants, which is an emotion.

To a Harvard graduate, it may mean the pay or appreciation is so little that they feel they can't live on it. To a vagrant, the hours they would be required to work may seem too long or deprive them of the freedom they have come to enjoy by having no possessions. Everyone has a reason for doing things, and when you ask why of your desires; you then begin to tap into the power of not only obtaining them faster, but enjoying the process along the way. "Why" gives you the reasons to move forward or to turn back from your goals. This is where true success begins. It moves a goal from desire to fruition. This is why success is "easy" to obtain.

Acting Upon Your WHY Instincts

This book has been chock full of useful tools and exercises for helping you obtain the success that you deserve, and by this time I would hope that you may begin to notice how ***Success = Life***. It's when you begin to notice these things that the success you want becomes visible to the one who matters: you. Within that newly acquired confidence, you can then begin to find answers that will make you successful. Successful people aren't different from you and me; they just utilize their emotions in a different way.

Those who are successful know what they want and why they want it. They know the power that comes from determining the emotional payoff before they even make any attempts at the goal itself. This emotional payoff is another use of the 10% Solution. Because if you have 10 ways to reach a goal and you are happy or satisfied with each step or way, then obtaining that goal will be possible for you.

For instance, can you tell me how many things in life right now that you enjoy doing? Whether your answers include hobbies, sports, or hanging out with friends', you would be able to give some convincing reasons, if I were to ask you "why" you enjoy these things.

Now, what if I could tell you that *you can get whatever you desire by doing what you enjoy...* wouldn't that be great? Then why don't you? By getting to the "why," you can do that.

Yet, before we get carried away with the idea that you can make a million dollars by drinking beer with your friends, you will have to understand what happens too many of the best ideas in the world. It's a silent killer that can even erase the best plans created by the most inventive 10% Solution. Please do the following exercise so you can learn to identify and eliminate this culprit from your life.

Exercise: Clarify your WHY

Take a few moments and do the 10% Solution, or if you have done so already, then go on to the next step.
Write a paragraph about *why* you want to accomplish whatever it is.

Now look at your ten solutions and ask, "Which are the best things that I can begin for free?" By "free," I mean that they cost very little or can be done with little effort- for example, making a phone call, research, or asking someone something.—Place a check mark next to those items.

For a moment take a break, relax and remember that any process for obtaining your goals should be done with *small easy steps that can be done for little or no effort.* Many begin their journey (as did and Dr. Robert Schuller) with little or no resources other than *a desire to succeed.*

So, if your goal was to make a million dollars, look at the solution list and notice those things you can do for little or no effort. These are things might include phone calls, researching on the Internet, or calling Kayton and having him do a 10% Solution for you (just kidding).

Most times, what occurs next is that these small "free" items *remain on the list.* Nothing happens. No calls are made, no letters written. No one decides to send Kayton a check for $500.00 to create a 10% Solution list for them (not kidding about the check). Your own life is a reflection of this, no doubt. Have there been times when initiating any plan meant making one small step and you put it off? Was it a trip to a library to begin that term paper? A matter of mailing that stupid envelope back to Ed McMahon so you could be visited by the "prize patrol?" Whatever it was or is in your life that has not been accomplished is the result of the question of "why" not being answered.

Procrastination, or the killer of ambition, is the result of not asking "why" of your goals. But if you procrastinate, it doesn't mean you are bad or lazy. You are simply doing what you have been designed to do, for without a clear picture of what we want and the emotional payoff we have attached to that goal, our brain won't let us move forward.

This happens because our brain isn't aware that the "goal" is what we desire. That "desire" part, of course, is an emotion and that is why it is important to recognize that "why" we want something is far more important than the simple wanting of it.

After all, the simple process of finding ten ways to solve a problem can give you answers which can lead to a step-by-step plan for achieving a goal but the plan will not work unless you do. If you don't decide the "why" to what it is you want, you won't follow through. That's a reality many have faced and will continue to face throughout their lifetimes.

Go back to the most recent exercise and apply "why" to the items you have checked as easy or "free." Ask *why* "I need to make this call or write this letter."

By applying "why" to each step or the idea of your main goal/situation, the solutions to your success become visible. This will happen because, for after asking yourself "why" (Why do I want this? Why can or can't I do this?), you will begin to see your strengths and weaknesses. From this perspective, you will notice that even though you have a great plan, you yourself may not initiate it if you don't enjoy doing some of the steps.

Why Not TO Do is Important Too

Sometimes discovering what we *don't* want to do is as important (if not more so) than what we do want to do in our journey towards success. In this moment of discovery that we can find the essence of who we are. It's this essence, this inner drive; most people never give a second thought about. Often they acknowledge *what they don't enjoy*, but never ask "why." Most assume and say, "It's just the way I am."

Why we don't things is a reaction that is derived from the part of our being which is here to protect us from pain. The pain can be real or imagined, it doesn't matter. What does matter is what we don't do in our lives that can make a difference in our outcomes.

The best advice I can give you is this. *Look at something you haven't done and ask the reason. Then try to describe that reason as a single word or emotion. Chances are, you will find, it will come back to something similar to the meaning of pain.*

After you have done this, celebrate! Rejoice in the fact that you are doing what exactly what most people do, which is avoid painful situations. Now take that "reason" from above and know that *you can find someone who enjoys what you find to be painful.*

An example, from my life, is answering the phone. I can't stand it. So, instead of just telling myself, "that's the way I am," I found someone who enjoys answering the phone and hired them! In a sense, my pain is their joy.

Also, don't get so caught up in the fact that you may have to pay somebody for doing something you don't want to do. When you ask, "Why you don't do certain things?" *the reality of the things you are good at will shine through*. Often you can trade these services with one another.

One example could be if you are good at writing, but hate public speaking, offer to be a speech writer in trade for a speaker to come to your event. Think of the things which you don't do and use the 10% Solution and "Why" to help you find those who will.

Each action of asking "why" has helped to shape what many of us call our "destiny." From that point or place called "destiny" you can then begin to understand the importance of the next chapter, which is about being.

Being a person who is focused on who they are and how that identity shapes their world is what we will learn in the upcoming pages.

Chapter 8

It's Time to *Be!*

There is an old saying that says, "We are not human doings but rather human *beings*." The emphasis comes across as we don't do things but rather are reflections of what we are being at points in time. For instance, say that you were "sad" about something. Maybe it was raining or you didn't get that pony for your birthday. Could others around you tell that you were indeed sad? Beyond friends and family, if a complete stranger came up to you, would they be able to tell you were feeling sad? Probably the answer is "yes."

While the reflection of sadness is unique to each person, there are universal signs that people show when an emotion is felt. If you were to describe what someone who was "sad" looked like, I feel confident that you would. I get that confidence from knowing that we as humans have so many emotions we can feel. These feelings, though we may have thousands of ways to describe them, are limited in their scope and how we feel them.

In chapter 5, we touched on this with the examples of pain and ecstasy or even happiness and sadness. It was said that if you took the essence of a certain emotion and were to describe it, the differences would be in the individuals' interpretation. This interpretation is the one key element that you need to become aware of as it relates to your own success. Many times at my seminars, I get to meet several people who are nice but can be perceived as being "mean" or "mean spirited." Other times I will meet "nice" people about whom I felt I couldn't trust with the most innocent of secrets. The point I want to make is that we all tend to judge others on the basis of face value. We judge others on their looks, but then when they "do" something to us or towards us, they "become" some type of label.

If someone steals your car, they are a "thief" (or a repo-man). When a man sleeps with another man's wife, he is an "adulterer" (or some other colorful term). The combination of a person "doing" something, combined with others' perceptions, creates what many would say as that person is "being," even if it is far from the truth! That is how I once was, by everyone's terms, a "success," while inside I was a failure. It explains how it is that when celebrities fall victim to suicide and overdoses, many fans are shocked and exclaim, "How could they *do* that? They had the world wrapped around their little finger!"

But if we sit back and try to see how others lives are affecting ours, we miss the point that we are the ones who are in fact control of it all. We, you and me, control our own thoughts, our own feelings and how we allow those feelings to influence our lives and those of the others around us.

This point is best illustrated in any grocery store on a Saturday morning. Keep an eye out for the "stressed" out parents. You will recognize these people with their baggy eyes and pre-mature gray hair and somewhere in close proximity to them will be one, two or more hellions running around. Many of them will be asking, *"Mom or Dad, can I have this, huh, can I, please?"*

After a period of pleading and reasoning by the child that "they deserve" a treat or toy, the parent usually gives in and says, *"Okay."*

From that example, the child is rewarded for being what they are. What I mean is that if you were to ask the child, "Why did you get that treat?" many times they would respond with an answer such as "I was being good". The same may hold true as a response from their parent as well. At some level, the parent either recognizes that a., the child was being good or b. the child was being persistent and the parent knew that a treat would shut them up. However, maybe the end result from the parent's perspective was not to "silence" the child's demands but to show their kids that they did deserve something. Whatever the case, the result is that *through consistent action a person is able to persevere and get to what they want.*

Success Side Note 24- *through consistent action a person is able to persevere and get to what they want.*

Acting in a certain manner helps determine the rewards that will be bestowed. If someone is being "bad," most times they will be punished. For a child it may mean going to a room without dinner. As an adult, this could mean a prison sentence or having to deal with my ex-wife.

What we decide to "be" at any moment is what we at some level become and others will perceive us as. This "be-coming" happens as we receive feedback from our actions. This feedback is a feeling which attaches to that or those specific actions. If things are "good" or we have good feelings about an action we are producing, we then associate action with feeling good. From that point on we will also identify ourselves with some part of the action. Here's an example to explain this.

Sex. The type of sex I'd like to discuss is what is called *"great sex."* For the sake of argument, let's say *"great sex"* is when one person creates a sense of ecstasy for another. I mean "no faking," but real life sweat-making, body-shaking, earth-quaking undeniable, unbridled passion. Get the picture?

Now that I have your attention, what do you think a person who could do this would consider themselves to be? In other words, if you or somebody you know could "rock" a person's sexual world, what do you think they would call themselves?

Some answers that I have heard over time from others are: "Don Juan," "I'm the MAN", "Pimp daddy", "John Holmes", "great lover." In one case, I even heard "orgasm facilitator!" These examples show that we classify names and our identities with the corresponding appropriate action.

You see, it's pretty likely you wouldn't stand up during an office meeting and proclaim that you are an "orgasm facilitator." Nor would you be at dinner with your parents and profess that you were a "great lover." No, these things would be left for the bedroom or some drunken discussion with your frat house buddies.

So, what does this have to do with you being a success? Well, I want you to think about how many times in your life were you successful at something? I'm not talking about making a million dollars or finding the cure for cancer, but those little things in life that you were successful at. Take a few moments and write them down or think about what they were. If you need a little help getting started, read this:

- Asking a person out on a date
- Tying my shoes
- Riding a bike
- Sleeping alone
- Sleeping with someone
- Convincing someone to do a task for you
- Getting a raise
- Getting hired

- Getting married

Your answer lies in the times you were successful at other things. Inside the answers of your own past, what is important is not so much what you were doing when these things transpired but the person you were *being.*

If you realize the essence of "who" you were being at the moment you experienced some of your life successes, you then can repeat that action. *Inside each of us are patterns that we have utilized to gain levels of success that our current lives reflect.* From the way we talk, the words we communicate with, and onwards to the seemingly endless things we do, each of us has a unique pattern for success and a pattern for failure.

Discovering those patterns can be done with reflection or by answering these questions: If in this moment you decided to be "successful", what would you do? Would you walk a certain way? Live someplace different from where you reside now? What kind of person would you *be* if you had everything you desired?

When you answer that last question, write it down. *Who or what kind of person would you "be" if you had everything you desired?*

Now think about an emotion that would relate to that successful person you would be? Have you figured what the emotion might be? Is it something along the lines of feeling happy, grateful, or secure?

Whatever your emotion is, why do you feel it is contingent upon your "ultimate success"? The easiest way to create lasting success is to see what you want to get from "being" a certain type of person and experiencing those feelings in your life *right now*.

In this universe do you realize we are the only things that can go "backwards" in time? I mean really, time itself is always moving forward. Light, moves from one point forwards through the universe to another point. We, through the illusion of what we call reality, are moving forwards like the rest of the universe, but in our minds we can relive or go back in time to another place. Most people who have gotten so good at it, they live each moment like it was yesterday. For those and the rest of the world that is, a good understanding of the Rule of success should be noted.

Remember the rule goes Success=Life, Life=Success. *You don't have to wait for the so-called things of success to happen before you experience the feelings associated with them*. In other words, take what you hope to get from being successful and begin to live each moment *as if you already possess it*. Once you begin to do this, over time you will get what it is you want.

Be in a "Place" of Control

Have you ever noticed that the most successful people in the world seem to be calm, even when all hell is breaking loose around them? What is their secret? It is simple.

The secret of attainment (in both of terms of success and calm) gets back to what was said about *perception* at the beginning of this chapter. When I asked you to remember some of your past successes I want you to realize that the way you pulled those things off was from a place of "being" in control. It was from this state of "being" that your perception of yourself and that of you by others helped create your success. This same state of "calm" is no different that one of "out of control". It gets back to and goes forward from a place of perception. Your perception of the moment at hand.

When you begin to think about any state of being and focus on it, you will then get to experience it. That is why so many look at their pasts or go back in time- it's familiar and they feel they control it. You have at times been successful. You have lived life, therefore you have not failed. You reading these words are a testament to life, *your life*, and even though you may not have the "success in a certain area that you desire yet," you do have the keys to create that success.

Where to find these keys? In the past of your own success as well as the success of others. It has been said that "success leaves clues", good cliché' but I prefer to say that "success leaves strategies", and strategies are what you want if you'd like to not have to struggle for success. Struggling for most is not being in a place of control but more like a small boat being tossed around in heavy seas. Stop taking on water and begin to look at the success you want by using your perception as the sail towards safe and richer shores.

If, for example, you wanted to make a million dollars (which for many equates to success) and the most you have ever done is convince your spouse to marry you, then look at that situation for what it is and create the steps for influencing the procurement of your new goal. How? Begin by doing a 10% Solution and then look at your past success (in this example, getting married) and remember the state of 'being' you were in at the time. The truth of any marriage is that one person, in a state of being, has to convince another that it is a good idea. That state can be called many things, love, adoration, committed, but I want you to understand less of the labeled emotion and more of the actions or strategies of the moment.

What did you do to propose? Did you plan it out? Did you copy someone else's idea?

That's fine for the married people, but you may be saying "I'm single". Okay then, look at something common to you, for instance the place you live. How did you get there? Did you look in the paper, drive around looking? Have a friend or roommate call you or maybe a relative? What is the strategy you used to get into this place you call "home"?

Being is a place of control reveals the strategies that you use and that others use as well. It's those strategies that can give everything you want, they already do. This book is an example of that.

When it came to writing it, the first person I had to convince was me. Then, I had to convince my wife. Then I had to find a literary agent who was interested in my work. Despite an entire stack of "no's" I got from prospective agents and publishers, I never stopped convincing the one person that needed to stay on board with this idea: *me*. What was my strategy?

You see, I knew I had to convince one person that my idea (I.D.E.A.) was valid and valuable to others. By first convincing myself and then by staying with that conviction, I decided to be a **Best –Selling Author.** Being a best-selling author in my mind meant doing the things I had to do to make that happen.

Strategy One- Convince myself, keep myself convinced that I was going to succeed.- I did this by placing notes upon my work area, making small sign that said Kayton B Kimberly- Best Selling Author, I even went so far as attending the *Blue Ridge Writers' Conference* with a name badge that said Kayton B Kimberly-soon to be Best Selling Author.

Beyond that, I lived my life everyday as if I had experienced what "success" had brought to me. In other words, I was in a state of *being*. What else did I do, persistently write or work on this book every day. Even if it was one word, one sentence, I did something, anything.

Strategy Two- Created the reality before reality- Once a month, letters telling people I had already written this book were mailed when in fact it was still sitting on my computer no where near complete! I didn't wait for things to happen before proclaiming I was a "best-selling" author. In my life, I was being *what I wanted to be*. Was I crazy? Depends on who you ask, I guess. But I was not going to "wait" for time to tell me otherwise.

Those Two Strategies, plus many I utilized from others who have done what I wanted to do are in a sense what have placed these words before you. Let me propose this question to you.

Can you tell me the exact date and time you will have the "success" that you want your life to have? I mean, can you say with any certainty at 3: 00 p.m. on August 26th you will become a millionaire?

Your answer should be "yes," if you begin *in this moment* to <u>become a millionaire</u>. If you decide to be what it is you want to experience, then you will have it. This is somewhat the opposite of what many of us are taught.

As children, many of us were taught to work. Often were asked, "What do you want to be when you grow up?" Many adults instill in children that being a doctor or a lawyer or some other profession are "noble undertakings" (fancy words for a "job"). That's because we want to make a significant difference, whether we're children and adults. It's a human trait, to want to be an individual in what we do. As children, we would idolize those adults whom we see as someone special. Remember playing house or doctor?

Why do we forget to "be" what we wanted to be from childhood? Most (the 90%) get busy *doing* instead of *being*.

Somewhere between hide 'n go seek and finding a job many of us (myself included) bought into the idea that getting a "job" was the responsible thing to do. *Wrong.* Remember that *what or who you want to be provides the insight into what you want to do.* That means you need to be responsible to the greatest person in the world; you. Success comes from this point. It comes to those who decide to "be" what they want to be and do the things they want to do. From personal experience, I can attest to the power of this.

For over 18 years I "did" what many by cultural standard deem to be the most dangerous job in the world: I was a "repo-man." You know, the guy that sneaks around in the middle of the night taking back things? It was the equivalent to a modern day Robin Hood, except my profession asked we take from those who couldn't afford things in the first place. But I was a "successful" repo-man.

I didn't get shot or even shot at. I was able to make a lot of money. I had all the "trappings" of success, but those very trappings made me *feel* trapped! I didn't feel successful even though, by the standards of others, I should have. The reason for this was simple. *I hated what I did.*

Then as a natural progression of things, I "self-destructed." I went from having it all to having nothing in less than a year. Why? It seemed that because I hated what I did, I hated myself.

Yet breaking away from your limitations to success is actually easy... I just didn't know it at the time! It comes from remembering back, and becoming the person, you *want* to be. "Being" then brings forth a new identity. From starting fresh and uncovering your true character, you can see that a *job becomes a means to fulfill a vision, and not the other way around.*

To get closer to success in your life, figure out what you wanted to be when you grew up. Ask yourself the question right now and write down the answer to, *what I wanted to be when I grew up.* Now take a look at your life as it is today. Are you being what you had wanted to be when you were a child? What is your job? Why do you do it? I know the obvious is to make "money", but beyond that. What feeling do you get from your job? Think about your childhood again. What similarities in the feelings of what you do now can be compared to what you wanted to be? Are there any?

Probably there are a few. When you get to the person you wanted to "be," then the ideas of what you do become relevant. Again, each of can earn money, it is not that hard. Go "flip burgers or dig ditches," as my dad used to say. Making money is a derivative of what we do. So is volunteering. *We earn our place in this world not by the money we make, but by the lives we touch.* It's called value. <u>The more value we create, the more we are paid. That is what success is.</u>

If, as a child, you wanted to "be" a doctor but aren't one today then look not at the actual position you hold but the feelings that you associate with it. For example, do you find that you help others in your current job? Do you fix things? Isn't that what you thought as a child you would "be" or "do" as a doctor?

Remember from Chapter 3- we define

Work = what enhances our life

Job = what puts money in our pockets.

For me, I knew growing up I wanted to help others. I enjoy it, and it's what I do best. Somewhere along the way, I picked up the idea that taking cars in the middle of the night was a way of helping others. It did help my clients and my friends in the business and I would often joke that we were "helping" people out of their cars. Yet I wasn't truly buying the idea. That's why I would cringe at the thought of answering the question of "what I did," for inside I couldn't stand being a repo-man. Why? I was doing what I had wanted to as a child… help others, right?

Half right.

Yes, my desire to help was being fulfilled (that's why I did it for 18 years), but I wasn't helping *those whom I wanted to help*. After a close self-examination, I concluded that I wanted to help out those whom I was taking the cars from. After all, growing up I had stood up for the little guys. I had saved birds and lizards. I released the tadpoles that my brother took all day to catch. The more people or creatures I could help, the better I felt. That was, and is, my inner core, and since I have tapped into that, I have reached the "success" my life deserves. I have become a Ten. That is what Tens do…that is what you must do.

Take the time to get clear on who you are. Stop doing for a minute and start *being*. If you get nothing else from this chapter then remember this word, behave. By taking the word and separating into two individual words, the secret to success is revealed. What ever you decide to "Be," then you will "have". The Tens decided to "be" successes so they "have" it. The 90% are still doing what they *think* will bring them success. You can do or you can be, but there is no such word as "do-have." You have to *be* first and then you will *have* what you want.

The time to ask is now, *do I want to keep doing the things I know in my heart won't bring me success, or do I want to be a success?* Answer it with care, and know inside that you are making the right decision. In the next chapter you will be exposed to an easy, practical way of getting the success you deserve.

Kayton Kimberly

Chapter 9

Beginning the Five steps: Attracting success

My hope is that by the time you read these words you will have decided on at least one thing in your life that you want to change. Before you start the process, however, you may find it helpful to do as I did: Admit the areas of weakness you have and utilize the five steps for finding someone *whose strength is your weakness.*

One of my largest weaknesses was feeling as if I had to do everything. I only realized after years of struggling and modeling others that, if my company was going to grow, I would have to "give up" some of the responsibility to others. This was one of the hardest things I ever did.

On a personal level, I felt as if I were "weak" and a "loser" for not being able to handle everything. I had been taught that "real men handle things." These were all perceptions, misperceptions!

But finally, I mustered up the nerve to hire somebody, and that's when I realized that *the hardest person you may have to ever convince is the one who looks back at you in the mirror.*

My life didn't begin to "work" until I had done this. It is hard to have a life if you are consumed with other things going on around you. Noted speaker Tony Robbins once said to me, *"It's impossible to drive into your future using a rearview mirror."* That was a perfect example of how my life was until I utilized the 5 steps to find someone whose strength is my weakness.

I was stuck in gear, always looking back at what everyone else was doing and giving no time to myself to create a future that I wanted. So I did what you are doing right now: I picked up a book with the hope and desire to find the answer to creating that future. I wanted off the treadmill of mediocrity and into the fast lane of success. I wanted someone, anyone to explain to me a step by step process for getting me to where I wanted to go. The reality of it all is that each and every book, tape and seminar I read, listened to, or attended frustrated me. I got close to the process for success but there was nothing there that I could apply to my life every day. Frustrated, I realized why these programs don't work.

Many are designed to teach others the way the author wants them to be taught. So many people get caught up in trying to sell others on the ideas they have that they forget that each of us are individuals. We may all be the same in biological terms, but who we are is as unique as a snowflake. I have different goals than you. You may like doing things that I find less than enjoyable. We all are different. So learning a way to success can't be universal… or can it?

Can many people learn how to get the success they want and have it last? I submit to you *yes*!

Yes, you can, and yes, you can teach someone close to you the same process for getting what he or she may want. This is accomplished by taking the individual idea of success and breaking it down to manageable sections. Then each section is utilized on a day-by-day basis.

Success comes from planning and doing, not from reading and talking. If you have in fact done each of the exercise that were asked of you prior to this point, then the five steps that follow will bring more focus and energy into your life.

Begin by getting the following: two sheets of blank paper and a pen. This is where we will lay out the foundation of what the 5 steps are about. On the first sheet of paper write the following leaving a space in between each area to be filled in with the appropriate answers: name, address, employment, creditors, and references. Take a moment and fill each area. Write down your name, current address, and current employer (or if unemployed write that). In the creditors area, write down who you owe and why. Is it on a car or credit cards? Do you owe your family any money? Write it down. Fill out the references as if you were asking for the biggest loan of your life. Now for references: who would you want someone to call upon?

So how do you look on paper? Be honest. If someone were to ask you three years ago where would you be, would it be at the address you have listed? Are you working for a living or living your work? Take some time to look at your "success application" with the understanding that this reflects a *point in time*. This is you today, not tomorrow or yesterday, but right now. This piece of paper with your information on it is where you will begin your journey to success. Now lets move on to the next step.

Set the first piece of paper aside and on the blank page write the following (leaving space in between the areas so they too may be filled with the appropriate information): Title, Where I Live, What I Do, Potential, Partners.

For the Title section, think about *who you like to be*. Answering these questions may help.

- How would you like others to think of you?
- Would you want a title like "millionaire" or "famous"? Maybe it is a professional title like doctor, lawyer, or disc jockey. How about syndicated disc jockey or world renowned doctor?

Get the picture?

If you could be anything or want to be recognized, what would that title (or titles) be? That's what you want to write down in the **Title section.**

Next comes, **Where I Live.** Write down whatever area you want, whether it's oceanfront or amidst the desert. Maybe it's a country or different state. If money were no object, where would you live? Capture the essence of the place where you want to live and not where you reside now (unless you are happy with your surroundings).

Now what is your fantasy job? The kind of thing that you can't believe you get paid for it because you love to do it so much. What have you always wanted to do but were told all the excuses of why you couldn't? Forget those feeble minded souls and write down your ultimate job. Is it becoming a rock star? The President? If you are having trouble, pretend you are 6 years old again and an adult has asked you want you want to be when you grow up. Or think of the worst job in the world. What would you *hate* doing? Now think of the opposite and that's your dream job. This technique also works well for relationships (think of the worst and then the opposite).

Potential. Saying the word almost brings about a sense of promise that an action is about to occur. In this area I would like for you to capture a few of your strengths. Are you a "nice" person? Do you help others? Have you done something remarkable that has brought you success in the past? We all have great potential to do everything we want in life, but many of us don't. (Well, that's not for lack of potential, but lack of a plan. And you are getting closer to having that plan.)

Now we move on to **Partners.** Let me start by mentioning an old quote you have heard several times before: "No man is an island." There is no exception. We all share this planet and our neighborhoods. For an "achiever" like me who wants to do everything, this is a real hard concept to understand. If this is a hard concept to grasp, then read on.

My guess is that if you are reading these words right now you didn't chop down the tree that made this page. Nor did you create the ink. Move beyond the simple words of this book and look at yourself. Did you wake up today and make your own clothes? How about the electricity that powers the lights you are reading this book by? What did you eat today? Did you have to grow it or hunt it down? The answer is probably no; these things were provided for you by someone else. Those "others" are your <u>partners.</u> We *all* have partners throughout life, partners who can help or hinder our success. Even if you think you don't have any partners right now, know that you do, for you wouldn't even be alive to read this without the love of a partner (be it a parent or sibling).

So who has you best interest at heart? If you are single and feel "alone," then write down yourself. There is another cliché' that says *you get what you give.* Well, if you want to have a partner and feel you don't have one now, then become a partner with yourself. Think of those around you and question if they have your best interest at heart. Make sure you move beyond "people" and think about *partners* in life. What I mean is ask yourself, am I getting the best rate on my phone bill (the company is one of your partners after all)? How about insurance? The cost of being alive often creates partners that may not be the best for us. But partners are also your friends. Do they want you too succeed? Write down a few names of partners with whom you like to be associated in the future.

Now take out both sheets of paper that you have filled out and place them in front of you, side by side, with about a six inch gap between them. Here now becomes a picture of your life. On one side is the present. On the other are your future and a *gap in between separating you from your future success*. What are the differences in where you want to go from where you are now? Compare your current name to the ***Title*** section. Do you feel better with the title you want to assume as your own or are you happy with your name?

Go to the next section and compare your address to ***Where I Live***. "If a man's home is his castle," are you King Arthur or one of the servants? Now look at your employment status as opposed to ***What I Do***. What will it take to get that dream job?

Consider both your creditors and your ***Potential.*** Your current status is a reflection of your potential. If you have great credit, your potential has been utilized to repay those debts and as a result, you get a good credit rating. If on the other hand, if you have seen better days, don't worry, because you have the same-potential to get what you want and to surpass it.

Compare your references to your ***Partners*** section. If both sections have the same names and you have not quite gotten the results you want in your life, and then re-evaluate whether these people or companies have your interest at heart. And realize that *your current references are a reflection to the person you will become.*

It's time to slide the two sheets of paper together, closing the gap of where you are as compared to where you want to go. Take a few more minutes and compare the two sides of you. After a few moments take both sheets and place them back to back, with one side facing up and the other facing down. Secure both sheets together, giving you your present on one side and your future on the other.

One of the biggest problems I had when doing this exercise was forgetting what I had accomplished along the way to getting my success. The combining of the sheets gave me a reference of where I had come from. It so easy to forget the great things we have accomplished in our lives if we don't have a record it. Now that you have done this, let's create a way to utilize these 5 steps that will bring forth the success you want.

If you'd like a blank copy of your Success Application, go to www.RepoYourLife.com and download a copy for free.

Chapter 10

The Five-Steps for Lifelong Success:
How to keep your success flowing!

This is "where the rubber meets the road." You have determined the success of your life. With any luck you have discovered there are at least ten solutions to each challenge. You realize that there might be something to this word "be-have" or *behave*. There may a sense of certainty that you can bridge that six-inch gap of who you are now and the person you are destined to become in the future. Well that certainty is the fuel that will forge the real you into reality. Follow along in each of the five steps. Each is designed to build upon the success of each moment we are given.

The Five Steps In Action

What you will need: Some type of time management tool, from the simplest (a calendar) to a day –planner. (For the sake of ease, I will refer to any time management tool as a calendar.)

Find a quiet place and grab the "success application" you created earlier along with a calendar. On the calendar fill in these words on the Monday thru Friday dates for the next 4 weeks, as follows.

- Under Mondays put "Title."
- Tuesdays, "Where I Live."
- Wednesday, "What I Do.
- Thursday, "Potential."
- Friday, "Partners."

Then at the top of the calendar write the following question: *What is one thing I can do to be a success in each area?* With that done, I want to sum up this entire process for you before beginning to use this process for change. Please set down your calendar and read on for a moment.

How the five day plan works

Neither success nor failure happens in one instance. If you try something once and it doesn't work, it is not a failure. *It is a result.* On the other hand, if you do something once and are successful, that too isn't a success. *Again, it is a result.* In all cases there are a series of events (or results) that bring these things we call "success" and "failure" into our lives. Those results help to shape our lives and our destiny.

Think about it. Did you grow up all in one day? Nope. That, my friends, took years of growth. Those years can be broken down into days, weeks, hours, minutes, and even seconds. The same can be said for all areas of your life. Take finances, for example. How many stories have we all heard of lottery winners who win millions of dollars too only go broke after a short period of time? Are they successful? I submit *yes, these people are successful*. Why? They in fact did what they have always done (lose money). Like them, we pick up these "habits" through-out life and they become the things we know. In essence, everything we do in life is what we know how to do.

Success comes to those who *are doing what they know instead of knowing what to do*. The difference between successes and those who aren't there yet is that what we call "bad" behaviors, or the things we feel we would like to change, are happening at a subconscious level. And at that level we lose our better judgment and do what we feel is right. In other words, many times we don't think with our heads but react with our hearts.

In this modern world of multi-tasking and high tech devices that are supposed to make our lives easier we are stressed out of our minds. We are sold a bill of goods that says *when everything else goes right in your life then you can have success*. However, a million dollars isn't the sum of who you are. Neither are computers or cars. You are successful at *being you*. There is nothing wrong with "blowing a million dollars" as in the example of the lottery winner earlier. Success means being the real you *and not making excuses for it.* If you are say "financially challenged" and are happy being broke, then that is being you. However, if you are doing something and you want to change, then you are not being you, but are becoming the person *you would like to be.*

Remember that laughing something off with the word, "That's how I am" is just an excuse. It is a crutch that people use so they don't have to do anything about themselves or a problem that exists. Excuses come from not understanding that the emotions of our life control who we are and what we do.

Think of your life as a scale. On one side you have all the good traits and thoughts about any subject area. On the other are the negative thoughts about that same subject. If there is balance between the two, your life will seem to be running okay, but the minute the emotions of good or bad are heavier in either direction, an imbalance happens. From the imbalance comes "im" (the first two letters), or "I'm." From "I'm" come the excuses: I'm too old, I'm not rich, and I'm not smart. Do you see a pattern?

Here instead is some positive "I'ms." I'm good looking. I'm beautiful. I'm rich. Who determines if you are happy are sad? You do. Who determines if you are rich or poor? You do. So, in the example of the lottery winners, who spent the money? They did. To some people spending money and being broke may make them happy at some level. *Sounds strange, but 'tis true.*

On the other hand, we as humans have a unique gift that allows us to create situations that may not be true. From these situations we create ideas about ourselves as well as others. If you feel that you can't manage money (or any other part of your life), take notice that it may be you alone who can feel that. No computer, or even these 5 steps, can change the way you feel (good or bad) about anything in your life. The hope is, though, is that by utilizing these 5 steps *you can change any part of your life that you want to be changed.*

It may sound like hard work, and for some it may be in the beginning. Yet by doing each of these steps daily, you will change your life one step at a time. It won't be a question of how, but a decision of when. Let's get back to our plan and begin the five step process now.

DAY ONE *Monday: Title*

Every Monday for the next four weeks is your Title day. Think of the Title you want to assume as your own. Now answer a results question (which you'll do for that day of the week): *What is one thing I can do here to be a success?* Here's an example I use in my life.

Under Title, I decided one aspect to being a success is to be a great husband. So *Great Husband* is my title for *Monday.* Next, I utilized the 10% Solution when it came to results and thought of ten different ways to show my wife that I'm a great husband. From those possible ways, I selected something easy that I know I can accomplish. With a busy schedule, I find that something that is easy for me to give is sending flowers to my wife. For my calendar for Monday I write Title, Great Husband, Send/ Pick up flowers. Then I do the obvious: I send the flowers. That is it. I'm a success.

The point to this is that I don't spend all day consumed with worrying if I am getting success in my life. *By planning and doing one or two small things that are focused towards an overall goal, I achieve success in that area of my life.* It's simply a matter of breaking things down into manageable chunks. That becomes the great secret to *getting your success.* Taking steps towards your success in a way that is thoughtful and repetitive will bring what you want to you. There is a no more effective way.

DAY TWO *Tuesday: Where I Live*

Again answer a results question: *What is one thing I can do to be a success in this area?* Consider whether the actual space you occupy is a reflection of the person you want to become or someone you'd like to forget. Where we live is an important reflection of how our lives are lived. In many cases, it mirrors what has been holding us back from success. So sometime in the near future take a walk through your current neighborhood and notice a few things (FYI, if you're at a loss for ideas, utilize this as your first step towards obtaining your goal in this area). Take note of the homes-that are well-manicured. Outside they appear clean and crisp. Notice the cars at these homes and see if they too reflect the same cleanliness. If you get a chance, keep an eye out for the owners. See how they are dressed.

If you live in apartment complex, notice the outside of the doors. Are they dirty and greasy with fingerprints? Do the children leave their bikes and toys outside for anyone to take or worse, be injured by? Again, locate the "clean" areas and notice those who live there.

You can use this test in any neighborhood. My prediction is that about 10% of the homes or apartments in that particular vicinity will stand out as "clean" by the rest of the area's standards. Now, do you belong in that 10% or do you see these homes and remember that you are not the most organized person and somewhere think, I *wouldn't be able to find a thing? Remember; it's important to be honest with you.*

A favorite saying of my wife, when we were house hunting was, "I don't want to have to clean all of those rooms." Can you see how the saying of that over and over again, would deter someone from moving into a larger home? A similar statement may have held you back in the past from gaining success in terms of being in a larger home.

So on Tuesday, make a note for one or two things you'd truly like to accomplish in respect to where and how you live, and *do them*! If you decided after a walk through your neighborhood, that you wanted your home to appear more beautiful on the outside, do a little thing like buy a flowering plant for your front stoop. Or, if you've decided you're unhappy with your neighborhood, but some homes in a nearby area strike a chord with you, do a big thing like call a Realtor®.

Day Three *Wednesday: What I Do*

Step 3 (Day 3 Wednesday): "This job sucks" was a motto of a dear friend of mine for about 4 years. Every day he would get up and drive to his big job in the city where he would sell insurance. His lunch hour (which was 20 minutes, for it took 40 minutes to get out of his office) would be spent eating in haste, when he ate at all. His wife never saw him except on weekends, and even then, he would sleep or sit on the couch dreading the arrival of Monday. He hated the fact that everyone thought he was an *insurance salesman* instead of this great guy that he in fact was. When I would ask him, "Why you don't quit?" he would respond by saying, "The payoff is around the corner." "I've invested too much time to give up now."

My friend had bought into an idea that wasn't his. He was led down a road believing that success took long periods of time to accomplish, and that you have to pay your dues in order to get to a great reward. After 4 years my friend came to a seminar I was having and got the gist of what I had been saying all along.

He realized he had gotten into the insurance "game" because a friend of his had made a ton of money there, and he thought it would be a great way for him to have a life of "success." My friend saw the payoff of residual income being the key to escaping his jail, rather than realizing making money in that fashion was, for him, a jail in and of itself. What my friend hadn't asked himself was, "Do I *want* to do this, or is there something else I can do that can generate the same idea income?"

So, are you doing something now that doesn't fit your needs, but you're too afraid of giving it up to get what you want? If you answer "yes," then ask and answer this question: *"Are you secure in your job or in your talents?"*

Wednesday's action is What I Do. This becomes the day to *act upon those thoughts you may have forgotten about, or not realized when it comes to your "job."* If you are happy at what you do, then determine one or two things you can do today to make your job even better, if not for yourself, then maybe for some else in your office. For those of us who are happy at what we do then consider sharing your expertise with others. Offer to train those with similar jobs at your location. If you want a change, then capture and act upon some things that you can do to pursue your "dream job."

Use the 10% Solution to create a list of other things you can do to create an income. Maybe it's something part-time or helping someone else in a similar field (trade off clients or team up for sales?). What ever it is or becomes, know that you are the one that determines your future, and no one else. If you have ever been "fired" from a job, go back and thank that person for opening up your career opportunity. Who knows, in a short time you may find yourself doing what my friend did which was call in "sick" to work. Here's what my friend decided to do...a pretty brave (and big) move indeed! My friend ended up calling in sick to work.

The conversation went as follows: *"Yes, Ms. Receptionist, I'm calling in sick today. The fact is I'm sick of working there so I won't be coming back. Tell the boss I'm sick of him, and I'm sick of the guy in accounting who has no idea what he is doing. In fact, I'm sick of the entire office. Have a nice day."*

Day Four *Thursday: Potential*

Thomas Edison once said, *"If we all did the things we are capable of doing, we would literally astound ourselves."*

I could write an entire book about human potential and great "comeback" stories. In its pages, I could tell of those who had a challenging card dealt to them and became greater than they once were. I want you to consider how different your life would be if you were doing things to your full potential. Because the fact is we, all know at some level we aren't doing things to our full potential.

That is one reason why you are still reading this.

But don't fall into the "big trap" that most other "self-help" programs try to sell you on. The trap snares you right when you believe those famous words that every infomercial proposes: "It's so easy, *anybody* can do it."

That's a trap because you aren't anybody; you are *you*. Your potential is yours and yours alone. I would like for you to understand that potential is nothing more than what you are good at. A great example is basketball star Michael Jordan. Now would you say he has the potential to do anything the wants? Sure. (By the way, we all have that same potential). Well, how about the time he decided he wanted to play baseball instead of basketball? Without discrediting Mr. Jordan, I will say that his performance on the baseball field had a lot to be desired. So why couldn't he play baseball, if he is, in fact a great athlete? Well, without getting technical, Michael Jordan's natural talent is in *basketball*. He has trained himself to utilize a different part of his brain that is effective on the court, not on the field.

Here's another example that's much closer to my heart, and it has to do with Algebra. My potential in Algebra was lacking, and boy did my grades show it. That lack of understanding in algebra caused a lot of aggravation in my life and made me think I was not as smart as I thought I was.

All of that changed in college, when I had a great instructor who could see what I *was* proficient in: art. He took me aside the first semester and told me that when it came to algebra problems, "It's ok to *draw* the problem." So that's what I did. I'd draw a little train going one way and another going the other way. I'd make a line graph to figure out the equation, and the correct answer would come to me like magic. It was his insight into my potential that made the difference. I later learned that I was a visual type of person. As long as I can draw or see the result I'm after, I can figure out a way to get there.

I can't be Michael Jordan or Michelangelo, but I can determine what my strengths are. Being "visual" is one of my strengths. What is yours? This is the day to find out. Your potential is unique. You own your strengths. Discovering what you can do is what today is about. One way to get there is to answer this question: *What are the core things you are good at?*

Take a few minutes and write down the answers. Next answer this: *How can I use my potential in every other area of my life?* This includes those areas you would like to "improve." You see I (with the help of a good teacher) was shown how to use my potential in an area I thought I was weak in (algebra). Decide to use the knowledge you've gained to handle a few of the challenges you've been putting off because you thought you didn't understand them enough to be good at them.

With practice you'll improve so don't think of your challenges as some huge undertakings that will never get done. Something's aren't so easy that everybody can do them right away, but maybe you can do them! Focus your strengths on the challenges to try to overcome them. Do this every Thursday until you master them, and then move onto other growth challenges.

Day Five *Friday: Partners*

People like people who are like themselves. Look at your current friends; are they a lot like you? Even if you have no friends, think of the people you appreciate, even if they are celebrities you admire. Do you believe at some level they have the same "character" as you in some way? By "character," I mean do you like the way certain people do certain things, and can you relate to them? The answer is "yes"- trust me, its biological instincts to like those whom are like us in many ways. In plain English, it's the nature of nature.

If you don't believe me, look no further than out a window and notice how nature itself is a partnership. A tree, with its roots deep underground, provides pathways for moles, and worms to travel. It keeps grass from eroding away. Its bark provides shelter for small bugs; its branches house nests for birds and squirrels. Those same branches give off oxygen, the stuff we humans need to breathe. We can even then take down a tree and make into other useful things, such as paper or wooden planks to build homes with.

That is one example of how a seemingly simple object like a tree creates partnerships during its life cycle. Now think of how many partners you have in life. Your friends, family, and loved ones they are all your partners. Anyone that you have a relationship with, a lover or a company is a partner. You may not know it, but at some level, you are giving them "power" to help shape your life.

Have you ever done something for someone else to make them feel better? I believe we all have at least once. Well that "power" comes from this need to put others in front of ourselves for the sake of what we may call "consideration." Consideration, the times when one opens a door for another, or says that a newborn "is the cutest baby ever" (when the kid truly looks like a lizard). Its part of the Golden Rule: "Do unto others as you would have done unto you." Be nice, be kind, don't cut in line, share, - all of these feel-good rules that have been instilled into us by whom? Our partners, that's who! So where do these partners come from? Well, perhaps the best answer includes responding to "why." Why do we have these partnerships? In part it's due the power of love.

Love is such a strong emotion, yet many don't take the time to realize how much we do for this thing we call "love". We do 95% of *everything in our lives* for this one emotion. If you are alone, you yearn for someone to be with. If you are with somebody, you want to provide for them. All of this comes from the emotion called love. Yet, as with any emotion, there are different levels, forms, and intensities.

We have a different "love" for our siblings than we do for our spouses, for our friends than for our families. The "love" emotion creates friendships just as it creates marriages. It creates families and holds them together, and perpetuates the generations of lives before and after us. And from all of this love floating around, partnerships are created.

Here is an extreme example of why I say love creates "partnerships" in life. It's "fictional" story of Bob and Sue, but is true in so many ways.

Bob meets Sue and they marry after three years of dating, because they are in "love". Now Bob is a successful banker and Sue a computer programmer. The first few years of their marriage are great. They both are making money, buy a little house in the suburbs; each has a Volvo, and is living the American dream. Isn't love grand?

However, one day Bob goes to work and surprise! He gets laid off. He comes home and tells his loving wife the news but isn't worried; he knows there is something "out there" for him to do. Sue makes him dinner gives him a massage and assures him everything will be alright. At this point, their love for each other is not even a question.

A week goes by, no job offers to be had by the by the once proud banker. "No problem" says Sue, "I know you will find something." Bob too agrees and they continue to have a wonderful life. A month goes by, with still no job; Bob cashes in some stock to "get them through." Sue begins to worry a little. Bob begins to worry as well. The marriage that was once full of afternoon talks and dinner dates is beginning to fray at the edges. Not because of affairs or of not loving each other, but because of all the partners that affect their marriage.

You see, without Bob's second income, these partners are starting make themselves known. There's the mortgage company that provided the money for the cute little house. The furniture store where they found that great leather couch. The power company, the phone company. The company that's responsible for Sue's cell phone. Then there is the insurance company, the company to which they are paying off two car loans on the Volvo's. Then there's gas and food. All of these are "partners" that many never even give a second thought too until times get "tough".

These partners have begun to make themselves known by calling and sending letters saying "we want our money." What has made the problem even worse is that, Bob feels that since he isn't providing, Sue may love him less. Now this may not be true, *but many times, we make things worse than they truly are and this is what Bob is beginning to do in his own mind.*

By the time three months have passed, Bob has let his partners get the best of him. Still unemployed, he sits at home, doing nothing and gaining weight, seeing in his mind the moment the repo-man will show up to take his Volvo. He doesn't answer the phone for he knows a bill collector will be on the other end. His mind begins to wander to all of the trips he and Sue took and the money he's "blown." He yearns to have half or even a fourth of what yesterday has taken. Inside he says, "If only" and then returns to reading the want ads. He searches for a job that will bring him back to where he was a loving husband with a great life, instead of a shell of a man that seems worthless.

He and Sue speak very little now. When she arrives home, she doesn't even bother to ask if he found anything. Sue has begun to go out with her friends, a justifiable reward for towing the line as she sees it. She wants to have a good time, not sit at home and be depressed with Bob. Sue's once a week girl's night out has turned into five.

You see, all of the partnerships that were created when Bob and Sue got together have now almost destroyed their marriage. Bob and Sue started having problems because they didn't understand the reality of partners. Yes, they loved each other very much, but so much that they went out and created a lot of partnerships that in the end created problems in their marriage.

The lesson I want you to take from this example is about creating and being with a partner that will be good for your success. So I want you to answer this question, Do I want to get my life in order and be a success? No doubt that your answer is "yes," so the first step in creating *great* partnerships is to list all of the current partners in your life. Start with your friends, your family, and co-workers. Next, write down your creditors and utility companies. Then consider your hobbies. Do you smoke? Drink alcohol? *Anything you use that is created by another is in essence a partner to you.* With list in hand I want you to first consider the person you feel the closest to (this could be your spouse, parent, pet or best-friend). Now, what do you do as a partner for this person you feel closest to? Do you work? Pay the bills? Provide shelter? Love them without question? I want to write down all of the things you do for this your closest partner.

Make sure to compare a lot of your current partners with what you are doing for your closest partner. Your creditors are the most obvious. Have you gone into debt for your partner? How about your current eating habits? Are they a reflection of what your closest partner does? I said earlier that we do 95% of everything for this thing called love. *Is this true in your own life?* Is the current list of partners just an expansion of your closest partner? Probably the answer is "yes." Now I would like to share with you some effective strategies for evaluating and creating partnerships.

Strategy One: Ask and answer these questions every Day 5, or Partner Day.

1) What can I do to be a great partner today?

2) If I were to lose it all, would this person (or partner) still be in my life?

3) What can I live without?

4) Is this partner getting me closer to my goals or keeping me away?

5) Who can I be a partner to today and help out?

Some of these questions may not be appropriate for every situation or partner, but by asking these questions of your current and future partners, you will begin to have clarity in your life. It's this clarity that will help you determine those who have your best interest at heart.

Strategy Two: Another key (or strategy) to evaluating the usefulness of partners in your life is writing down on paper what you don't need in your life and discussing it with your closet partner. Pretend for a minute you could start with a clean slate and determine what your basic needs are. If you have a home, clothing, and food, what wouldn't you need that you have in your life right now? Of all the current partners you have, how many would stick with you through anything? Could you get rid of some partners that may not be the best for you at this time? To help you with this process, separate your partners into three groups: *Partners we need, partners we have and partners we don't want.*

- *Partners we need.* These are spouses, family, closest of friends. To determine who or which partners go in this column, think of people who would miss you if you were to die tomorrow.

- *Partners we have.* Figure out why they are there in the first place. Make sure they complete your life in some way. Your book club or the person at the store whom you always chat with goes into this grouping. You want to include casual friends, creditors, and stores. You job or employer can go here as well (unless you feel you need your job).

- *Partners you don't want.* You didn't wake up one day with a huge debt or three car loans to pay off, so get creative figure how to make these a better partner or more valued partner in your life or send them on their way. For example, you can't easily get rid of the IRS, but getting a good accountant to help you maximize your deductions would be a great way to make the IRS a better partner in your life.

Now that you have completed these groupings, you can see what you need to get rid of (partnership-wise) and where you need to build your strengths. If you have many partners in the "partners you have" category, ask the 5 questions and determine if you need them or if they are partners you don't want.

There is also one other thought I want to share about partners. *Partners are what make the four other steps work.* I mean, what good is your "title" (day 1) if there is no one to share it with.

"Where I live" (day 2) would be an empty place without a partner.

"What I do" (day 3) is meaningless unless it inspires or helps someone else.

Day 4 "Potential" could not be measured without the efforts of partners around you. Napoleon Hill wrote about "mastermind alliances" in his book *Think and Grow Rich*. He discusses how of all the things accomplished, from inventions to new ways of doing business, none were done by a single person. *Needing others is a fact of life.*

Yet, in many cases it is the people we surrounded ourselves with who may have helped to keep us from where we want to be. This was true in my own life. I mention this not so that you will go out and blame someone else if you're not where you want to be, but so that you will remember to make sure that there's clarity in your life. <u>The clarity to see life for what you want it to be and not what others want you to believe. The clarity to attract and keep success in your life.</u>

Applying the Steps Successfully to Your Life

The five steps we've just covered *will do nothing for you if you do not apply them to your life.* They will however, change your life *if* you have faith in yourself and if you do each step day by day. But don't try to re-create your world in 30 days or even 7. Take a small step each Monday through Friday and do one or two little things to get you further on your path to success. If you remember nothing else from this book, take this away- **The biggest successes are the result of many baby steps.**

Tony Robbins summed it up by saying, *"Nothing has any meaning except the meaning you give it."* If you did something once and didn't get what you wanted (or what many call "failure"), know that you got a <u>result</u> and that my friend is <u>something</u>. This book came from my desire to have "meaning" in my life and it is my hope that by reading this you can "get busy living…" and having a life that means something to you.

Chapter 11

Beyond today:

As you find yourself here at the end of this book, I feel it's important to share what I call "life benefits." Life Benefits are designed to enhance your life in ways you may have never thought about. Some of the things I suggest may not be new to you; others may be. But if you latch onto one technique, one new way of seeing things, who knows where that will take you? Life itself is an ongoing discovery, and something you try today may give you the gifts you search so long for.

Tip # 1- Get a Journal and Write.

I would love to tell you that writing in a journal every day will bring untold riches to you. But I can't. Why? Well, I have no proof of it. However, what I can tell you with utmost certainty is that a journal is a valuable tool.

Imagine for a moment if you could recall something great you did ten years ago. I know many of you are saying, "Gosh I can't remember what I did last week much less ten years ago!" Well I'm in that same boat as well, except I have a secret memory weapon: a journal from that period in time. In it, I immortalize some successful moments, which I can go to again and again.

Journals are not just for love struck teenage girls. Some of the most influential people over time captured their thoughts in journals. Ben Franklin and Thomas Edison to Fred Durst (of the music group *Limp Bizkit*) and Tony Robbins have jotted down important things in their lives. Things like their dreams and their desires. They gave themselves the gifts of remembrance. These offerings of moments passed are easily revisited by a simple the turn of a page.

So get a journal. Many are under $20.00 at book or office supply stores. Even if you write in it once a month, imagine what you will have to look over at the end of the year!

Journals are a wonderful place to house your thoughts, as in them you can explore even those ideas you find too embarrassing to express aloud.

Tip # 2: Take a Marketing Course (no matter who you are)

Next to a journal, I feel this kind of course is a necessary Life Benefit for every person alive. We are taught in our schools that reading and writing are important. We are also taught logical processes such as math. What traditional education doesn't cover is the one area that keeps every human alive: emotions.

An emotion, not logical thinking, is what "drives" us and marketing (or advertising) is what *"hooks"* each of us into taking action. This hook is achieved by accessing the emotional part in each of us, and then linking a product or service to it. By taking a course on the subject of marketing, you get to see how this process is done. And in taking, you also may learn a few things about yourself.

Even if you are not in the business world or feel you don't such a class, take one anyway. It is worth its weight in gold.

Tip # 3: Open a Business (even if you don't think you can)

Corporations are entities unto themselves that may help you keep more of what you earn. Incorporating (or creating a business on paper) is low cost when compared to the tax savings one can gain.

When you have a business (corporation, LLC or some other legal business entity) things that would otherwise be taxed to you are write offs to the company. Take gas, for instance. Many who don't have a business cannot take that as a deduction from their taxes. However, if you bought fuel during the course of doing something "business related", you can deduct that expense from your taxes.

Now I'm no accountant or lawyer, so check with a tax professional to see what the advantages of "being in business" for yourself can be. You may be surprised by the amount of money you can save or deduct by doing such a thing. Also, beyond taxes there are other discounts awaiting business owners.

Hotels and rental cars often offer a discount for business travelers: All one has to do is in the asking for it. Ask "do you offer a discount for business?" The same holds true for airline tickets and purchasing items from "discount warehouses." As of this writing, you also can get free business cards for your new company at www.vistaprint.com. Yes, being in business for oneself does have its advantages!

Tip # 4: Give things away

This is the something you've probably heard before. Don't disregard the cliché that goes, "You get what you give." It's true. *What ever it is you want, give it away and it will come back to you.* Now for many, the desire is to have money or some other thing of value. That is a great goal to have. But when were the last time you gave away something that you wanted? Like money, for an instance?

Most people I meet tell me with a certain amount of conviction that when they make a million dollars, then they will give some to charity. Since few will ever make a million dollars, many of us find a void in our life exists because we never then give away things (in this case, money) we wanted too.

If you want something, give it away, but here is the secret: *seek out the essence of what it is you want.* By doing that you will find you can give "it" away in a different form and yet what you want will come to you that are of the same essence. Want an example?

Back to the money issue. The logical thing to do is to give money away, and then money will return, right? Well that's great if you've got it to give. But what is the essence of money to you? Freedom? The social stature it will bring? A way to expand your world? Whatever its **_essence is_**, find a way to give **_that_** away. If it is freedom, then take someone for a car ride. Write a letter to a prisoner. Both are ways to help someone else experience freedom. By giving that away, you will get in return what it is that you want.

Tip # 5: Go to a Seminar (never stop learning)

Seminars are great places to meet like-minded people. You can make friends there who will last a lifetime. Beyond the social aspects of seminars, though, you can learn a few things. As we grow-up, the thought and desire to learn is dissipated in the need to survive. Many exclaim that "they don't have time to learn or go to some seminar; they've got bills to pay." I know; I've said it once or twice in my life too. But some of the most exciting moments and greatest discoveries I uncovered about myself were at seminars.

Also, if you are pursuing Tip # 3 (open a business), you may be able to write off the entire thing as "continuing education." So the question becomes, what costs more to you, ignorance or experience?

Go to a seminar. Many offer money- back guarantees or better yet, there are plenty of free ones out there as well. Try them.

Tip # 6: Get a pet.

Pets are great companions. Most will show unconditional love and help bring about a sense of routine that we as humans need. Some will say that they are allergic or don't have the time for an animal in their life. Well, as for the allergies, I have never heard anyone who is allergic to live fish. As for the time, I can appreciate that confession, since I'm a jet-setter as well, but that still does not let you off the hook.

Adopt an animal at your local zoo or help out with a rescue in your area. Rescues go beyond being a "pound" or a last stop for stray animals. Many are breed-specific, so if you can't own say an English Mastiff, you can help out those who care for them adopt these lovable huge dogs.

My wife Danielle made me "guilty by association" when she told me that "we" were volunteering for a Boxer Rescue. Needless to say, it too has been one of the more rewarding points in my life. I've been able to help others see the fun and adventure of Boxers who were, for a time, wanted no more. I was also able to share in the love of some great dogs. Even if you are unable to care for an animal in a direct way, send money, food or small gift to help out those who can't speak for themselves, but love each of us no matter what we do.

Tip # 7: Get a Massage

Getting a massage is a two-fold event. One, it helps you to relax and rejuvenate from what the world takes from you. There is also something about the human touch, which is soothing and peaceful, that gives you time to think. Second, it helps your body detoxify.

Check your local yellow pages for this spa service, or better yet, ask someone you know for a referral. Remember, people like people who are like themselves, so if your friend recommends a particular massage therapist; chances are you will enjoy them as well.

Once you find one, don't be afraid to tell them what you expect or what makes you uncomfortable. Also, check into other types of relaxation like hydrotherapy and acupuncture. You may find that being relaxed once a month or once a week is your ticket to finding lasting success.

Tip # 8: Read a book or two

This is one of those things that people take the wrong way. Often I am told that people read enough by picking up newspaper; so why should they read a book? Experience.

Newspapers are written so an average 6th grader can understand them. There is no challenge, no adventure. The news doesn't stimulate your mind. It's like reading a memo at work. What's in a newspaper is recycled information making its way to you.

But with a book, you can experience what the writer wants you too. You can explore another world or learn something new. You can relive a time that you weren't even born into. You can do all of this and more from your favorite chair.

Books make life richer for those who read them and for those who write them. Don't deny yourself one of the great rewards of life.

Tip # 9: Exercise

You knew that one was coming. But instead of me telling you how or when to exercise (there are plenty of others who can do that), let me propose a question to you. *How much better is your life when you feel good as opposed to bad? Is there a quantifiable difference?*

When we feel good, we work harder and longer. Life seems to flow along smoothly. As we know, the opposite is true as well. When we feel bad, we work less and getting out of bed can seem impossible. Yet, with exercise (and proper nutrition), finding "I'm possible" from impossible happens in an instant.

The hardest part about exercise is getting started. The next hardest part is following through. Eliminate both of the "excuses" by getting a buddy or hiring a trainer. Also, design a routine that fits you and your lifestyle; don't try to follow the "packaged coach" from off the shelf. What I mean here is the plethora of videos and latest fad workouts. Incorporate what you like to do with exercise into your routine, and you will do it.

If you like walking, then go for a walk. If you enjoy reading a trashy novel, then get on a stationary bike and read. Do what's fun and you'll do it more often.

Tip # 10: Be Grateful Every Day.

Cultivating a sense of gratitude towards everything you have is the last tip I have for you. If you can develop this habit, your world will expand beyond anything you can ever dream. I have done this, and it has brought me to such new heights that I wish for you to master this tip as well.

Practicing gratitude does take some work. After all, when are we most thankful? For many, it's a holiday in November. But to get a sense of true thankfulness, one needs to practice at it more than once a year! Gratitude needs to become a habit everyday, from when we first wake up to when we fall to sleep.

Gratitude arises from taking advantage of the things we have the most control over: our thoughts and our actions. We can choose at any moment to be happy or grateful. We are born with the essence of choice, the essence of decision.

By reading this book, you have in fact done what many others just dream about. You have used your power of choice to expose yourself to the thought of taking your life back. If you have done any of the exercises or, better yet, committed yourself to utilizing the 5 day plan, you are well on your way to *Repossessing Your Life.*

It has been my honor to share these thoughts with you. I wish you the best from what our universe has to offer, and I look forward to meeting you in person someday. Until that moment, thanks, and remember: only *you* can **Repossess Your Life!**

Other Resources to seek out:

If you would like some great resources, please check out information and products offered by these great teachers and information sources.

Also check out **RepoYourLife.com** or **KaytonKimberly.com** for additional resources including products, seminars and other life changing happenings.

These are in no particular order:

Steve G Jones (Hypnotherapist)   www.SteveGJones.com
Tony Robbins (Life Coaching)   www.TonyRobbins.com
Suze Orman (Finances)   www.SuzeOrman.com
Jim Rohn (Motivation)   www.JimRohn.com
Deepak Chopra (Spirituality)   www.DeepakChopra.com
Brent BecVar, M.S. (Vedic Counseling)   brentbecvar@aol.com
Claudia Holton (life coaching)   www.coachingromspirit.com
Dave Ramsey (living Debt Free)   www.DaveRamsey.com
Dan Kennedy (marketing guru)   www.DanKennedy.com

About the Author

Kayton Kimberly is a native to south Florida. When his father decided to leave the banking industry and open a repo- business, Kayton was there repossessing his first car at fourteen. While other boys his age were "chasing girls", he was finding *dead beats* who were trying to skip out on paying. When he reached the age of twenty, he opened his own agency, and found great success in the repossession business. His business grew from a one man operation to a multi-office, million-dollar plus producing company. In 2001, his company was recognized by PRIME, Inc, for excellence in the Collateral Recovery Industry.

Throughout his career, Kayton has consulted with many Fortune 500 Companies including, *BMW Finance, HAFC, CarMax, First North American Credit, Mercedes Benz, Land Rover, and Ford Motor Credit*. He has appeared on *The Dolan's syndicated Radio show*, contributed articles to the *Wall Street Journal* and *Professional Repossessor Magazine*.

Mr. Kimberly has also instructed courses for the *State of Florida* and continues to share his positive message through live seminars and audio programs as well as through *www.LearnToRepo.com*. He lives in Florida and Michigan with his wife Danielle, 3 Boxers, and Boston terrier.

You can contact him at many places including, www.KaytonKimberly.com, www.RepoYourLife.com or at www.myspace.com/kaytonkimberly.

www.ingramcontent.com/pod-product-compliance
Lightning Source LLC
Chambersburg PA
CBHW061322040426
42444CB00011B/2727